# Critical Thinking and Professional Judgement for Social Work

**Other titles in the Post-Qualifying Social Work Practice series**

# Critical Thinking and Professional Judgement for Social Work

## Third Edition

**LYNNE RUTTER AND KEITH BROWN**

Series Editor Keith Brown

Los Angeles | London | New Delhi
Singapore | Washington DC

Learning Matters
An imprint of SAGE Publications Ltd
1 Oliver's Yard
55 City Road
London EC1Y 1SP

SAGE Publications Inc.
2455 Teller Road
Thousand Oaks, California 91320

SAGE Publications India Pvt Ltd
B 1/I 1 Mohan Cooperative Industrial Area
Mathura Road
New Delhi 110 044

SAGE Publications Asia-Pacific Pte Ltd
33 Pekin Street #02-01
Far East Square
Singapore 048763

Editor: Luke Block
Development editor: Kate Lodge
Production controller: Chris Marke
Project management: Deer Park Productions
Marketing manager: Zoe Seaton
Cover design: Code 5 Design Associates Ltd
Typeset by: Pantek Media
Printed by: Bell & Bain Ltd

First published 2006
Second edition published 2008
Third edition published 2012 (previously
published as Critical Thinking for Social Work)

British Library Cataloguing in Publication data

A catalogue record for this book is available from
the British Library

ISBN: 978 0 85725 753 6

# Centre for Post-Qualifying Social Work at Bournemouth University

Welcome to one of our publications to support students undertaking post-qualifying learning.

The various books have been specifically designed and written to support students and we hope you find them of value to both your study and practice of social work.

The texts have been written by experienced practitioners and are therefore up to date with issues for social work practice.

*Professor Keith Brown*
*Director of the Centre for Post-Qualifying Social Work, Bournemouth University*

# Contents

# Foreword: A series to support post-qualifying social work

This text, *Critical Thinking and Professional Judgement for Social Work,* is one of a series of texts written by experienced social work educators and practitioners, some of whom are working at the Centre for Post-Qualifying Social Work at Bournemouth University.

All the texts are written with the specific aim of supporting social workers who are undertaking post qualifying studies in their chosen field of practice/specialism. However, much of the content of each text is also valuable to students on qualifying social work programmes.

As members of the Centre for Post-Qualifying Social Work, we all work with the aim of promoting the best social work practice for the sake of all service users and their carers.

I trust that you will find this text of real value in your social work career.


*Professor Keith Brown*
*Director of the Centre for Post Qualifying Social Work*

# About the authors

**Lynne Rutter**

Lynne holds academic and professional qualifications in librarianship and education. Currently she teaches practice/work-based learning, and provides academic support via tutorials, and printed teaching and learning materials. Lynne has an MA in academic practice and is in her final year researching professional education and learning within a professional doctorate programme.

**Professor Keith Brown**

Keith holds professional qualifications in nursing, social work and teaching; and academic qualifications in nursing, social work and management. He has worked in the education and training field for over 25 years, working for three universities and three local authority social work departments. Currently he is the Director of the Centre for Post-Qualifying Social Work at Bournemouth University. In 2005 he was awarded the Linda Ammon Memorial Award, sponsored by the then Department for Education and Skills, a prize awarded to the individual making the greatest contribution to training and education in the UK.

# Preface to the third edition

We have been delighted with the responses to the first two editions of this text and especially to hear that students and social workers have found it valuable in their studies, and in reflection of their practice.

We decided to produce a third edition in order to take account of recent reforms and drivers in social work education. These include the Newly Qualified Social Worker Frameworks developed by the Children's Workforce Development Council (CWDC) and Skills for Care (SfC); the Social Work Reform Board's (SWRB, 2010, 2011) recommendations and proposals for a Continuing Professional Development Framework aligned to a Professional Capabilities Framework (PCF); as well as certain recommendations from the Munro Review of Child Protection: Final Report (Munro, 2011). These reforms and proposals will impact on post-qualifying education but perhaps more importantly they also firmly prioritise the continuing development of a social worker's professional capabilities. In respect of this, we have not only made necessary minor changes throughout the text, we have also included a new chapter, 'Professional judgement', which aims to offer some insight to support a critical approach to the development of professional judgement and expertise, and amended the title of the book.

We are more than ever aware that there is much to celebrate with respect to social work practice. Social workers and social work students often work with great imagination and skill with vulnerable members of society. This text aims to assist you, the practitioner, to critically think about, reflect on, and express your practice in order to continually review and develop your expertise. We sincerely hope this text enables you to demonstrate and evidence your professional competence and capability, and enhances your learning and professional development.

*Lynne Rutter*
*Professor Keith Brown*

# Introduction

Critical thinking as a process can appear formal and academic, something far removed from everyday life where decisions have to be taken quickly in less than ideal conditions. It is therefore unhelpful to present critical thinking as a linear process or a set of techniques for everyday working conditions because we rarely have the time or opportunity to follow a strict order in our thinking. We have adopted a more holistic approach and therefore this work does not aim to be a textbook on critical thinking skills or theories. We do not aim to 'teach' critical thinking. Rather this handbook aims to act as a guide and resource, suggesting ideas from our own practice and the work of others to help you develop your own critical approaches to practice.

An important review (Phillips and Bond, 2004) found four different conceptions for critical thinking.

- As a generic skill.

- As an embedded skill.

- As a component of lifelong learning.

- For critical being.

All these notions are apparent within the circumstances and requirements of the social work degree and post-qualifying (PQ) learning. As learners and as students you require a set of initial generic and subject-specific critical techniques to work with, but developing critical abilities within the social work arena can also enhance learning and development and there is potential to progress your own style of critical thinking. Our concept encompasses the idea that critical thinking can be developed and embedded within existing practice abilities in order for a practitioner to deal confidently with an uncertain and ever-changing world.

Our ideas have been developed from practice experience with students over many years, and from our ongoing research and reading on the subject. In order not to interrupt the flow of ideas or detract from the informal style of this guide, we have kept referencing to a minimum.

## Structure of the book

The first chapter explores the many different ways this book can help qualifying and post-qualifying social work students as well as practitioners. In the second chapter we look at a useful conception of critical thinking as a set of 'requisite intellectual resources' (Bailin et al., 1999). These generic resources are explored further in the following chapters and are enhanced with more context-specific critical abilities, qualities and approaches appropriate for qualifying and post-qualifying practice. The book provides chapters on professional judgement, using knowledge in practice, critical reflection, writing, critical practice, and lastly on continuing learning.

This book takes a pragmatic look at a range of ideas associated with critical thinking and judgement, particularly those linked with learning and development. It aims to present a number of ideas which should assist you in initially developing your knowledge and abilities within your study area. You are all unique learners and practitioners working in very different professional contexts so we have included a number of questions and activities to help you develop your own ideas and perspectives on this material. If you wish to enhance your understanding further in a particular area you will find suggested titles for further reading provided at the end of each chapter.

## Third edition

This third edition has been updated throughout to take account of recent reforms and drivers in social work, such as the *Newly Qualified Social Worker Framework*, the proposed *Professional Capabilities Framework for Social Workers in England*, and recommendations by the Social Work Reform Board (SWRB, 2010, 2011) and the Munro Review of Child Protection: Final Report (Munro, 2011). As ever, it aims to provide help and guidance for post-qualifying learning but also aims to be of value to all social work practitioners and students.

A new chapter has been included to encompass the recognition of professional judgement in developing expertise. This chapter highlights and discusses the importance of practical reasoning for professional judgement and the ways in which it can be critically enhanced and developed.

# *Chapter 1*
## Who is this book for?

## How can the handbook help with qualifying and post-qualifying learning?

This book is written primarily for post-qualifying learners but there are a number of ways in which critical thinking, particularly when associated with reflection and experiential learning, becomes an essential part of learning and development on qualifying programmes and for all areas of continuing professional development. The aims and intended learning outcomes of such programmes and the requirements for continuing professional development show us how.

### Qualifying programmes

In 2003, professional qualifying training for social workers in the United Kingdom changed from diploma to an undergraduate degree level. Qualities such as working in complex situations, exercising powers and responsibilities, managing risk, and making informed decisions are all listed as final-year undergraduate assessment standards. These qualities involve various aspects associated with critical thinking, for example reflection and sound deliberation, which in turn enable the application and development of knowledge and skills in the workplace. This is particularly pertinent now that qualifying students are expected to complete a significant number of days' practice learning on placement. These placements are aimed at facilitating the development of social work skills, knowledge, critical analysis and evidence-based application of knowledge through work-based learning experiences. Developing critical thinking abilities and attributes can particularly help qualifying students extract and express in writing the learning and professional development occurring during their placements.

### PQ/CPD learning

It is important to note that with the closure of the GSCC framework of approved and regulated post-qualifying (PQ) courses, existing PQ awards will be offered within a new Continuing Professional Development (CPD) Framework. At the time of writing the Social Work Reform Board (SWRB, 2011) has proposed the set of principles that should underpin this CPD Framework, aligned to the *Professional Capabilities Framework* (PCF), which aims to help social workers develop specialist knowledge and improve their practice and progress in their careers. Mapping the aims, requirements and outcomes of current PQ awards against the PCF shows a good fit. The Munro Review (Munro, 2011) has stated that formal CPD programmes accredited by the Higher Education Institution (HEI) play a fundamental role in the development of social work expertise.

The new CPD Framework will be developed by the College of Social Work and aims to provide the structure and support for social workers to develop their capabilities through-out their careers – to update, extend and deepen knowledge, skills and analytical thinking to deal with increasingly complex and specialist work and to develop professional iden-tity and confidence. As post-qualifying development within the new CPD Framework will involve a range of learning and development activities, and take the shape of informal as well as structured learning, we refer throughout the handbook to PQ learning.

## Continuing professional learning requirements

Initial proposals for implementing a coherent and effective national framework for the con-tinuing professional development of social workers developed by the Social Work Reform Board (SWRB, 2011) include the following references to continuing learning requirements.

- *The framework will support social workers to maintain and develop core standards for re-registration set by the regulatory body, the Health Professions Council (HPC) from July 2012. (The HPC will be known as the Health Care Professions Council once the Health and Social Care Bill has been passed.)*

- *Social workers will be supported by employers and expected to take professional responsibility for developing their skills to a high professional level, through under-taking learning and development activities over and above the core standards required for re-registration with HPC.*

- *Learning and development needs will be identified, planned for and monitored through annual appraisal cycles and supervision.*

- *Mechanisms for recognising and recording CPD activities will be established to pro-vide clarity of process, and portability across the country.*

The proposals also note that:

*Social workers will be required to provide a self declaration every two years that they continue to meet HPC standards for CPD. Evidence of CPD will therefore be mandatory for those who wish to maintain registration and protection of title as a social worker. This is the minimum that employers will be expected to support their staff to achieve. The HPC does not define either the content or the amount of CPD to be undertaken for any of the professions it regulates; assessment of sufficiency is based on learning outcomes and not (as currently) on number of hours completed.*

*Criteria for re-registration include that applicants will:*

- *Have maintained a continuous up to date and accurate CPD record.*

- *Have accessed a range of relevant learning activities.*

- *Can provide, on request, evidence of how CPD has contributed to the quality of their practice and service delivery.*

- *Can provide, on request, evidence of how their learning has benefited service users.*

Social workers are therefore expected to take professional responsibility for their own and others' CPD, but employers are also expected to take their part in fostering a culture which values learning and development across the organisation, e.g. providing resources, time and access to learning and research, together with appropriate supervision. The role of leadership in developing and supporting learning cultures is apparent here. A wide range of learning and development activities and opportunities, e.g. in-house training, use of feedback and colleagues, supervision, reflection, case discussion, formal PQ programmes, need to be systematically recorded and recognised as contributing to CPD. The need for reliable assessment of the learning output and impact on practice is also apparent, in order to ensure appropriate evidencing.

As Rolfe et al. (2001) show, developing practice and learning is difficult to separate. The development of practice is an ongoing activity, it generates experiential knowledge and so to practise is also to learn. The process and outcomes of continuing learning, when meaningfully achieved, will almost naturally embed themselves into processes of working, for example with clearer thinking, writing and reflection. Appropriate evaluation of this learning and its impact on practice can ensure the outputs are fully recognised, recorded and accredited where necessary.

The most important learning, however, is meta-learning – that is, learning about how you learn – and this is the basis of lifelong learning. This handbook, therefore, also focuses on learning as an end in itself and makes critical thinking and practice an integrated way of continuing to develop.

# How can this book help with practice?

Social work as a profession has always demanded critical abilities and qualities from its practitioners because decisions have to be made 'on the spot' and under pressure. With practice situations being so complex the consequences of any judgements, decisions and action are extremely important. The practitioner is working with uncertainty, risk, diversity and difference in a way that recognises oppression, and works to empower and promote the needs and rights of users and carers. This requirement goes beyond 'competent practice' and demands 'critical practice' (Adams et al., 2002), and the development of 'critical being', i.e. a person who not only reflects critically on knowledge but also develops their powers of critical self-reflection and critical action (Barnett, 1997).

No matter what we do we cannot escape our thinking but it can often be left unquestioned in our busy lives. We suggest that developing critical thinking can ensure that we use the best thinking we are capable of in any set of circumstances, and continually refine our professional judgement and expertise.

# Chapter 2
## Critical thinking

Aspects of critical thinking are apparent when you consider, deliberate, assess, make decisions or judgements, and discuss or debate issues with others, so most social workers have plenty of skills and experience to build on. We are therefore not aiming to teach or present a set of separate techniques but to start you working with some relevant, generic ideas and principles which can develop your own style of critical thinking further.

We do not intend to cover the full range of critical thinking 'skills' but instead highlight a few basic principles to underpin the process of enhancing the critical aspects of your own learning and development.

## What's it all about?

Brookfield (1987) shows that critical thinking is a lived and creative activity, not an academic pastime.

*Being a critical thinker involves more than cognitive activities such as logical reasoning or scrutinising arguments for assertions unsupported by empirical evidence. Thinking critically involves our recognising the assumptions underlying our beliefs and behaviours. It means we can give justifications for our ideas and actions. Most important, perhaps, it means we try to judge the rationality of these justifications. We can do this by comparing them to a range of varying interpretations and perspectives.*

(Brookfield, 1987, pp13–14)

Thinking critically can therefore result in major shifts in our ways of thinking and the development of reflective scepticism, i.e. when nothing is regarded as a universal truth, or taken on trust anymore. Our assumptions and beliefs, the views of others, and existing structures all start to be questioned, no matter what their basis or authority. It is powerful and transformative stuff and the challenge can be extremely positive. However, critical thinking can also be threatening, provoke anxiety and create adverse reactions from other people. It is hard work, involving self-doubt and mental blocks, but for many it leads to more creative leaps and insights. If you find yourself being adversely affected by the negative aspects, we advise you to seek support.

Critical thinking should not produce cynics but confident people who can be committed to a point of view that is well informed, rational and supported by relevant and valid material for that situation, but who are also open to other ideas. These are the type of social workers the public deserve.

# How can it be achieved?

Because people vary according to their capacities, abilities and experience, how you think critically will be personal to you. To develop this individuality we need an appropriate theory to provide us with valid and useful goals, methods and outcomes, i.e. an underpinning framework and structure. We propose to initially approach the 'how' in our context by using the theory of Bailin et al. (1999), who suggest that the critical thinker can be thought of in terms of a set of 'requisite intellectual resources'. These ideas have also been used successfully by Ford et al. (2004, 2005) in their research on criticality with students in social work education, and are explored below.

The intellectual resources for critical thinking are:

- background knowledge;
- critical concepts;
- critical thinking standards;
- strategies;
- habits of mind.

We will look at each of these resources in turn and examine their components, why they are thought to be necessary, where and how they might be of use. We can also identify the ones we need to develop further.

## Background knowledge of the situation in question

Bailin et al. (1999, p290) propose that:

> *...the depth of knowledge, understanding and experience persons have in a particular area of study or practice is a significant determinant of the degree to which they are capable of thinking critically in that area.*

In other words, the more you know about a situation and the context in which it sits, the better. This includes existing concepts, beliefs, values and ways of acting, as well as the usual background information which helps clarify the range of available options, e.g. for assessment purposes. However, professional judgement is required to make an informed decision about the actual use of this material. Thus, 'context' plays a significant role in determining what will count as sensible or reasonable application of any standards and principles of critical thinking. This contextually sensitive and moral approach appears well suited to the social work arena and allows for responsible deliberation.

---

**QUESTIONS**

*You don't know what you don't know, so how do you ensure that you are not missing something important about a practice situation?*

*How do you find out more – who and what are your sources?*

---

## Possession of critical concepts

In order to deliberate responsibly, and appraise all the material or information we are presented with, we need to understand the ideas and language (the concepts) associated with critical thinking. It is too easy to limit thinking about practice to thinking only of practice – that is, we get wrapped up in the detail and specifics of particular cases and the associated decision and actions, rather than dealing with general underlying issues. For example, an individual practitioner may reflect on a particular judgement by reviewing the available data and decision trail but not realise that he/she was uncritically following the initial but biased 'team view' on the case. Indeed, in many situations general concerns such as the amount of time we have or associated managerialist pressures all reduce our ability to think as carefully and critically as we would like.

Understanding critical thinking allows us to become more aware of these underlying issues and certain natural human tendencies towards bias that we would normally not even recognise. This type of knowledge does run into areas of psychology and human behaviour but we do not need to study a new discipline here. For much of the time the key is to be able to dig deep enough and be honest enough to start to recognise the underlying but hidden beliefs, preconceptions and assumptions we have, or we are working with.

Many authoritative websites explain the range of relevant cognitive and behavioural biases. Here are a few examples.

- Anchoring effect – tendency to rely too heavily or 'anchor' on one trait or piece of information when making decisions.

- Bandwagon effect – tendency to do or believe things because others do.

- Confirmation bias – tendency to search or interpret information in a way that confirms one's preconceptions.

- Hindsight bias – noted by the Munro Review (Munro, 2011), distorts our judgement about the predictability of an adverse outcome. When we look backwards it seems clear which assessments or actions were critical in leading to that outcome and we overestimate how visible the signs of danger were.

- Outcome bias – tendency to judge a decision by its eventual outcome rather than the quality of the decision at the time it was made.

- Pseudo-certainty effect – tendency to make risk-averse choices if the expected outcome is positive, but make risk-seeking choices to avoid negative outcomes.

Critical thinking can be largely concerned with distinguishing and understanding various kinds of argument (e.g. Gibbs and Gambrill, 1999; Cottrell, 2003). Although this can be viewed as an academic and mechanistic exercise, it does allow us to realise how easily we form flawed arguments ourselves and accept those that others present to us. We can become more aware of how arguments work and develop the language to critique them properly rather than just 'feeling' there was something wrong with them.

For this part of the book we will focus on formal, logical arguments to initially show key features of the approach. However, it is fully recognised that informal, practical arguments and reasoning are also likely to form the basis of professional judgement and align with the complexity, uncertainty and contingent nature of work-based decision-making (Kondrat, 1992). For this reason we will critically consider them fully in the following chapter.

### *Logical arguments*

Before we can fully appraise a logical argument we first need to know which type it is, and secondly have a full understanding regarding its various parts to make appropriate distinctions and judge it. Logical arguments are used to suggest the truth or demonstrate the falsity of a particular claim. Logic is important because it helps us reason correctly – correct reasoning gives us a viable means for knowing the truth or arriving at sound beliefs. Logical arguments are composed of propositions that are capable of being either true or false, and can serve as the objects of belief – they are the building blocks. The propositions used as reasons/evidence within the argument become the argument's premises. They are the grounds for accepting the argument and its conclusion, which is also the final proposition. There is a movement from one or more propositions used as premises to the proposition argued for as the conclusion.

- This bookcase is wood – proposition/premise.

- Wood is a strong material – proposition/premise.

- The bookcase will support my heavy books – final proposition/ conclusion.

The premises must be true and 'accepted' and their relevance to each other and the conclusion must be adequately supported. Premises will differ in their acceptability and credibility, and therefore in their sufficiency to support the conclusion, and so they need to be critically examined. Any proposition also already carries with it other accepted positions, assumptions or 'givens' that are not always made explicit but which need to be critically examined. For example, a premise that states 'This country needs educated citizens to develop' will have a set of assumptions about what a citizen should be or do, and about the role of the education system.

The final proposition is arrived at on the basis of one or more other propositions already accepted or known to be true, and so it this connection or inference between them which is important in logical argument. The question is whether the truth of the conclusion follows from that of the premises. The problem is that inference, by its nature, is not explicit, but it does need to be examined. In the example above the inference could be that the wood the bookshelf is made out of is the right quality for the weight of the books.

### Types of logical argument – deductive and inductive

#### Deductive arguments

The appropriate logical sequence for a deductive argument moves from the general to the specific. A valid argument here is defined as one where the argument's structure actually works as a sequence, even though the propositions (as premises or conclusion) may be false. A sound argument is a valid argument whose premises are all true and so it always arrives at a true conclusion. Be careful not to confuse valid arguments with sound arguments.

*Example 1 – valid but unsound deductive argument*. One of the premises is false and so the conclusion is false. However, if the premises were all true then the conclusion would be true because the structure works as a sequence, and so the argument itself remains a valid one.

*Premise*: All tigers are blue.
*Premise*: The animal outside my window is a tiger.
*Conclusion*: The tiger outside my window is blue.

So it is important to note the fact that just because a deductive argument is valid, it does not imply that its conclusion holds true.

*Example 2 – valid and sound deductive argument.* The premises are true, the conclusion is true and the argument is valid and sound.

*Premise*: All pilots are people who know how to fly airplanes.
*Premise*: John is a pilot.
*Conclusion*: John knows how to fly airplanes.

*Example 3 – invalid deductive argument*. The premises are all true but the conclusion actually ends up being false and so the argument is invalid.

*Premise*: Fish can swim.
*Premise*: My father can swim.
*Conclusion*: My father is a fish.

How does this happen? It is usually because of the hidden inferences and assumptions we mentioned above. This refers to anything that is taken for granted, e.g. facts, ideas or beliefs, which underlie the argument. For a deductive argument to have a justifiable conclusion (be sound as well as valid) not only must its premises be true, but the inferences which underlie them must also be reasonable and justifiable. As we said, a deductive argument infers from the general to the specific. This is where the problem occurs because other factors in a general statement might be present but not acknowledged. Our example inferred that anything that swims must be a fish. We could have worded the proposition as 'only fish can swim' and then it would have been a valid argument at least, although obviously unsound.

Let's look at a more relevant example (from Gibbs and Gambrill, 1999):

*Premise*: John has an attention-deficit hyperactivity disorder.
*Premise*: This disorder decreases academic performance.
*Premise*: Drug x reduces hyperactivity in school children.
*Conclusion*: If we prescribe Drug x for John, his academic performance will improve.

---

QUESTION

*What are the inferences here?*

---

ACTIVITY *2.1*

*Write out a deductive argument using premises and conclusions from a practice example.*

*What are the inferences or assumptions?*

COMMENT

*Doing this should allow you to see how much an argument relies on its inferences to make the links between the premises. As a deductive argument works from very general premises to more specific ones it relies on a large number of inferences and assumptions which are naturally implicit. They obviously need to be made explicit and examined further to see if they are correct and relevant.*

---

**Inductive arguments**

An inductive argument usually argues and infers from the specific to the general, i.e. in the opposite way to a deductive argument. An inductive argument is one where the premises provide some evidence for the truth of the conclusion. Inductive arguments are not valid or invalid. This means that if the premises are true in an inductive argument then it is probable that the conclusion is true, but it might not be. Inductive reasoning consists of inferring from the properties of a sample to the properties of a population as a whole and works with the notion of probabilities.

For example, suppose we have a container containing 1,000 beads. Some of the beads are red and some of the beads are blue. If we take a sample of 100 beads from the container and 50 of them are red and 50 of them are blue, then we could infer inductively that half the beads in the container are red and half are blue. In all probability we are likely to be about right, but we could also be very wrong. Inductive reasoning also depends on the similarity of the sample and the population. The more similar the sample is to the population as a whole, the more reliable will be the inductive inference. No inductive inference is perfect and any of them can fail. So, even though the premises are true, the conclusion might be false. Nonetheless, a good inductive inference will give us reason to believe that the conclusion is probably true.

Many general medical and social work theories are based upon observations of very specific experiments with samples. In our deductive example one of the premises was based on such a theory: 'Drug x reduces hyperactivity in school children'. However, as we know, experiments cannot take into account all circumstances or situations (i.e. the evidence is incomplete). To see if this was an acceptable inductive conclusion in its own right it would be necessary to see whether the experiments with Drug x were tested with a similar sample of children to John.

In another child care context, Bowlby's findings (1951,1969) suggested that infants who were separated from their mothers at an early age had behavioural and emotional difficulties later. This was used to argue the case against mothers working outside the home. This conclusion no doubt suited the economic conditions at the time; however, the data was based on children in very extreme institutionalised situations and one could argue that these were not 'typical' children. So the conclusion may not have been justified even though the research was accurate. Research usually progresses in this way with later researchers questioning aspects such as whether the sample was representative or whether the research contained assumptions invisible at the time (Cottrell, 2003).

---

*ACTIVITY* **2.2**

*Do you know of any other social work theories that have been based on inductive reasoning? Why are they considered valid?*

**COMMENT**

*The validity of any theory is considered in more detail later in this chapter, but any inductively based theory would need to have undergone further research to show its relevance and use to a wider population from the one where it was generated.*

---

## Knowledge of critical thinking standards

Once the critical concepts (the ideas and language) are understood we need practical methods to help us be critical about something. We need standards that will enable us to deliberate and judge effectively. Standards of critical analysis and appraisal are specific for each area of activity, i.e. standards for criticising an argument will be different to those used for criticising a piece of research.

Critical thinking standards do not always guide a thinker on how to apply them. Their nature makes it necessary for the critical thinker to exercise judgement in interpreting them and determining what they require in any particular case. Which is how it should be if you think about it! The way in which you exercise this judgement and interpret the relevant standards gives you important material for discussion on your programme. The worst way to use them would be as unexamined tick-box lists. Developing such judgement is like learning a language – you don't follow an exact set of rules in speech, but you can act in a way the standards suggest (e.g. using unambiguous words and short sentences) and recognise when your thinking fulfils these relevant standards (e.g. other people understanding you, rules of grammar).

This is obviously a huge subject and so we have initially collated below the generalised standards relevant for the critical appraisal of logical arguments, which we focused on above. Further standards and principles for other aspects of professional practice, e.g. critically thinking about practical arguments, knowledge and reflection, are considered in later chapters. All these standards and principles obviously need to be kept under review to ensure they are appropriate for each particular context.

---

QUESTIONS

*Where do you make 'logical arguments' in the workplace?*

*Which standards or guiding principles do you apply to critically appraise them?*

*Have you come across any flawed reasoning or assumptions recently? How did you recognise and/or question them?*

---

### Critical analysis of deductive arguments (from Gibbs and Gambrill, 1999)

- Does the conclusion have at least one premise in support of it?

- Are all the premises relevant to the truth of the conclusion? A premise is only acceptable if it:

  - is a matter of undisputed common knowledge;

  - can be adequately defended;

  - is the conclusion of another good argument;

  - is an incontrovertible eyewitness testimony;

  - is an incontrovertible report from an expert in the field;

  - is different from the conclusion itself;

  - does not contradict the evidence, a well-established claim, a reliable source or other premises in the same argument;

  - is not self-contradictory, linguistically confusing or unintelligible.

- When viewed together, do the premises constitute sufficient grounds for the truth of the conclusion? – i.e. strong enough in number, weight and kind (small and /or unrepresentative samples, or anecdotal evidence would be considered weak).

- Do the premises provide an effective rebuttal to all reasonable challenges to the argument? This is a good criterion for distinguishing mediocre arguments, because many people ignore or hide contrary evidence. Good arguers examine counterarguments as well as compatible ones.

A deductive argument may be unsound because:

- there may be something wrong with its logical structure, e.g. when the conclusion does not follow on logically from the reasons preceding it and the inferences are weak;

- it contains 'false' (irrelevant, unacceptable, weak) premises;

- it bases conclusions on too little evidence (generalising from incomplete information) or overlooks alternative conclusions.

### Critical analysis of inductive arguments

- The size of the sample should not be too small to support the conclusion.

- The sample used should not be relevantly different from the population as a whole.

- Any analogies must be valid. (For example, it is argued that since A has property P, so also B must have property P. An analogy fails when the two objects, A and B, are different in a way which affects whether they both have property P.)

- Important evidence which would undermine an inductive argument should not be excluded from consideration. The requirement that all relevant information be included is called the 'principle of total evidence'.

## Knowledge of strategies

People discover or devise key strategies and procedures for guiding and critically checking their performance in a variety of thinking tasks, e.g. making lists of pros and cons for decision-making; using examples for clarifying terms; discussing issues with a knowledge-able person. Specific strategies tend to be more helpful than those designed to apply in all cases and each of us will have our own preferred methods and techniques. What is most helpful is when they are made more explicit and shared among people struggling with the same issue.

---

*ACTIVITY* **2.3**

*List some strategies or tips you already have for practice, e.g. making decisions, problem-solving; and for learning, e.g. reading, studying?*

*These ideas are great to share in groups – how can you create an opportunity to share ideas on your course or programme – over coffee, via e-mail?*

**COMMENT**

*Informal methods can be very successful ways to share ideas and ways of working with colleagues and team members, but it can also be productive to create a time within a more formal gathering so more people can get involved.*

---

## Habits of mind

As Bailin et al. (1999, p294) point out, having all the intellectual resources necessary for critical thinking does not make anyone a critical thinker. The final resource is probably the most important of them all. We need to have certain commitments, attitudes or habits (e.g. respect for reason and truth, an open rather than a defensive attitude) and recognise the value of critical thinking in fostering true belief and responsible judgement/action as well. These attributes are closely tied up with our ethics and values. Social work, with its interdisciplinary nature and its inherent value system guiding judgement and action, is obviously well placed for fostering such habits of mind, but it is easy to become complacent and believe they are occurring automatically. Chapter 7 looks more closely at how routine practice easily becomes uncritical and even arrogant practice.

In practice we need knowledge about the subject at hand, self-knowledge (an honest recognition of how we think and reason), plus a range of values, attitudes and dispositions related to personal humility, human rights and the dignity and intrinsic worth of all human beings. These attributes underpin the ability to practise critically and encourage the inherent requirements of social work: openness, questioning and responsibility.

---

**REFLECTION POINT**

*Which specific social work (or other practice) values do you think are relevant to critical thinking?*

---

# Review

We have chosen to use one set of critical thinking ideas to develop in this section but you will probably find other authors' work echoing this material. For example, Smith (1992) identifies three key factors in critical thinking: knowledge, authority and a willingness to doubt. 'Knowledge' fits exactly with our first intellectual resource of background knowledge; 'authority' would involve the use of our critical concepts, standards and strategies; and 'a willingness to doubt' would be our habit of mind.

As we can see, critical thinking cannot be thought of as something that finds perfect solutions. Rather, the skills and abilities of critical thinking allow the best quality decisions or actions possible for the situations we encounter. Our holistic view advocates not just the application of critical thinking principles and techniques, but a more developed understanding of how our thinking operates in our day-to-day environments and the dangers we need to become more aware of.

We have only focused on more formal arguments in this chapter to initially demonstrate the usage of these ideas. However, your PQ learning will provide many opportunities to use these critical thinking principles in undertaking professional judgement, using new knowledge in practice, in reflecting on learning and practice, and when writing. We will now explore each of these areas in turn in the following chapters and develop the notion of critical thinking within them.

**FURTHER READING**

**Brookfield, S** (1987) *Developing critical thinkers.* Milton Keynes: Open University Press.

A general but insightful look at becoming a critical person.

**Fisher, A** (2001) *Critical thinking. An introduction.* Cambridge: Cambridge University Press.

An excellent introduction for specific critical thinking concepts and techniques.

Research in Practice **www.rip.org.uk** (accessed 8.9.2011)

Research in Practice for Adults **http://ripfa.org.uk** (accessed 8.9.2011)

RIP and RIPFA promote positive outcomes for children and families, and for adults through the use of research evidence. Their learning resources concentrate on current research and how to apply it to practice and provide skills development opportunities for improving evidence-informed practice.

# Chapter 3
## Professional judgement

**ACHIEVING POST QUALIFYING SOCIAL WORK AWARDS**

This chapter will help you to meet the following National Occupational Standards for Social Work.
*Key role 6: Unit 18: Research, analyse, evaluate and use current knowledge of best social work practice*
If you are a registered social worker, this chapter will also assist you to evidence these areas of the Professional Capabilities Framework:
- Professionalism
- Values and ethics.

Professional judgement is now being promoted as a crucial aspect of social work expertise. The Social Work Reform Board (SWRB, 2010) specifically requires the CPD Framework to enable social workers' ability to exercise their professional judgement. The Munro Review (Munro, 2011) wants to help professionals move from a compliance culture to a learning culture where they have more freedom to use their expertise and judgement in assessing need and providing the right help. As the Review explains, prescribed procedures can deal well with typical scenarios but not with unusual ones, and an organisational culture where procedural compliance is dominant can stifle the development of such expertise. Procedures are incomplete in two key ways. First, they do not encompass the judgement necessary to apply them and take account of specific circumstances. Second, they are also unable to encompass the more tacit skills, knowledge and capabilities which make up professional judgement and expertise.

---

*ACTIVITY* **3.1**

*Note the range of professional judgements you make in practice. Which are prescribed by organisational procedure and to what extent?*

**COMMENT**

*This could obviously be a long list! It is interesting to note just how much of our own thinking, interpretation, reasoning and decision making is necessary to put into effect policies, procedures and day-to-day processes, no matter how 'prescribed' they are. Of course, such judgement is underpinned by the enactment of our morals and values.*

Professional judgement is also associated with accountable decision-making as well as risk assessment and management, and therefore with the ability to predict the future and manage risk of harm. Obviously, as the Munro Review highlights, there has to be a realistic expectation of professionals' abilities to make predictions about future harm and manage such risk. Such decisions are, and will always be fallible because human beings are essentially unpredictable – we cannot eradicate risk, only reduce the probability of harm. Any professional judgement process has to be based on realistic conceptions of human strengths and weaknesses, work with uncertainty and be as sound and robust as it can be. One way to manage this is to ensure the process is not only value-based but also openly subject to critical thinking. This, in turn, needs to avoid a prescriptive approach to practice and focus on professional learning and increasing capability and expertise. To take account of these issues an important but general aspect of professional judgement can now be identified and explored in more detail: reasoning.

An important point to note here is that for effective professional judgements to be made and have an appropriate impact, there also needs to be clear, value-based leadership exhibited by all practitioners. Recent cases of systematic abuse of residents in care at the time of writing (such as Winterbourne View) show how easily care without a clear sense of personal responsibility and professional leadership can become abuse. We would argue that people do not come into the care industry with a desire to abuse and in some cases torture clients – yet it is clear such abuse happens. The well-known phrase – all that is necessary for the triumph of evil is for good men to do nothing – comes to mind. Without clear moral leadership based on professional judgement, values and standards, a culture can develop where abusive behaviour is not challenged and becomes tolerated or a blind eye turned to it. Professional, moral judgement is clearly not in evidence in these situations. The key point we are trying to make here is that high quality professional practice encompasses individual leadership based on sound judgement derived from a set of professional moral standards. Every professional can take a lead to ensure that not only is best possible practice fostered, but a working climate is developed within which all those involved in care are clear that abusive practices of any form will not be tolerated.

# Practical reasoning

Judgement is said to be at the core of professional practice, and it is practical reasoning which is said to be a key part of this judgement-making process (Kondrat, 1992; Beckett and Hager, 2001). Of course, moral reasoning is also a vital part of social work practice and there is an important moral aspect to practical reasoning which we will see below. However, a full exploration of this topic is seen to be beyond the scope of this handbook at the present time. We refer you to several useful texts in the Further Reading section at the end of the chapter.

Making professional judgements and the practical reasoning this involves appears central to the idea of professionalism and reflective practice in general. Logical reasoning and arguments (seen in the previous chapter) are not dismissed, but the use of reason in a formalised, logical or theoretical sense to decide what to believe is not necessarily sufficient to decide what to do in a certain situation. Practical reasoning, because it is the use of reason directed towards action, helps determine how to figure out what to do and how to do it (Streumer, 2009).

We must be very clear that this is not about procedural problems where requirements are already established and the problem defined. As Reid (1979) states, practical reasoning is about:

- identifying the questions to which we must respond;
- establishing the grounds for deciding the answers;
- choosing between available solutions.

This deliberation involves the effective use of a wide range of knowledge and information to understand problems, define areas within which solutions can be sought and justify the arguments and judgements that guided the choice between possible solutions. It activates, critically appraises and interprets formal and informal knowledge, skills, attributes and values to this end.

In effect, it is about the desirability of certain actions from a professional's point of view. A sign of professional maturity is a shift away from decisions that are arbitrated by an external authority to one in which individuals provide their own justification for decisions, using their own and other's expertise (Kandlbinder, 2007). This aligns well with the fundamental essence of professional judgement – making sure the most sound and moral option is produced for the situation at hand and taking responsibility for that.

Practical reasoning works by encouraging an informed, explicit, moral and reasonable relationship between situational goals and actions; it therefore promotes a critically reflective, reciprocal dialogue between those means and ends.

One fundamental feature of practical reasoning is that there is no established process to it because it is happening in active, complex and evolving or uncertain situations. Practical reasoning, therefore, cannot be viewed or approached as a prescriptive list of rules to be followed, and if it starts to establish too set a path or imposes regulatory systems it becomes rigid and unworkable. Nevertheless, there are particular features and principles associated with practical reasoning. It is important that these are understood in order to make practical reasoning as good as it can be, and to allow an objective and critical evaluation of it where possible or necessary. Table 3.1 below presents the principles of sound practical reasoning.

**Table 3.1** Framework of practical reasoning principles

| Practical reasoning principles |
| --- |
| Situational appreciation, i.e. sensitivity to, and discernment of, the particular characteristics and features of a situation (including ethics, circumstances and needs). |
| Attention paid to the complexity and uncertainty of a situation, i.e. this is not ignored or overly reduced. |
| Transparent purpose and intentions, e.g. explicable aims/objectives. |
| Critical appraisal and interpretation of formal and informal knowledge, skills, attributes and values. |
| A clear exchange between the particular characteristics and features of the situation (e.g. a person's behaviour) and the wider context (e.g. social/cultural norms) in order to gain a fully informed view; as well as between subjective (personal) and objective (neutral) perspectives. |

*Continued*

**Table 3.1** continued

| |
|---|
| A moral and reasonable relationship is established between goals /objectives and resulting decisions/actions via a critically reflective, reciprocal dialogue between means (how we do something) and ends (the outcome). |
| Critical thinking is used within the process to:<br><br>• weigh up risks, options, pros and cons, contingencies;<br><br>• adjudicate between competing goals and demands;<br><br>• generate and deliberate between alternatives, choices;<br><br>• create review or monitoring points;<br><br>• take into account relevant constraints and limitations. |
| Outcomes, decisions/actions are prudent, appropriate and useful to the situation's needs, etc. |
| New understanding and meaning (expertise) is developed. |

---

ACTIVITY **3.2**

*Applying the principles*

*Think about a particular area of practice you have recently been involved with where you exercised your judgement. Use the details of this situation to make notes under each of the principles above and see how useful they are to help examine and explore your practical reasoning and the judgement you made.*

COMMENT

*The principles can highlight important aspects of understanding and working with situations in a rigorous way, but we can be restricted by the amount of time and information available to us – it will never be perfect! Nevertheless, becoming aware of the principles of sound practical reasoning can not only enable us to review and improve the information and processes we are working with, but also help us to recognise when the information or processes are inadequate, and we need to delay making a decision.*

## Further critical thinking about practical reasoning

As well as using the principles detailed above to understand and critically review practical reasoning, there are other significant issues to be aware of. The first is that deciding what to do, or what the 'best' thing is to do, will be greatly influenced by the presumptions, preconceptions and 'givens' within the situation, which, as ever, become hidden biases and prejudices being worked to. These may relate to local or national strategies or rhetoric, or to more personal beliefs. Posing questions right from the start can help us unearth and examine them before they exert their influence. A critical awareness of why what we have thought of as the best option is 'best' should be made explicit. The overall point is to raise awareness of aspects of ourselves, and our team, that are usually subconscious but which have the power to impact heavily on our thought processes and our more conscious reasoning, decisions and actions.

*Which questions might help uncover the 'givens' within a situation?*

This is not an easy task but the need is to expose what is already understood, accepted, perceived or expected. It will be more effective, therefore, if someone else questions us and plays 'devil's advocate' to determine the existence and validity of these positions.

The second issue is that it is not straightforward to establish what the best thing is to do, or the best way to do it in any situation, because we usually have limited and/or imperfect information to work with. This obviously affects our ability to achieve the necessary situational awareness which underpins effective practical reasoning. Establishing a critical awareness of what information or understanding is lacking can be a key part of the learning involved in any situation; looking at how to address such deficiency in the future increases the potential for developing further expertise.

# Judgement statements

In practice we may be called on to make quick judgement calls, or a brief summary of a situation in the form of statements. These types of statements can be defined and explored briefly here to understand their nature and critically consider them. It may be that the type of language we are using is not suitable for the impact or outcome needed, or we may wish to challenge someone else's statements.

Here are some brief examples.

- *John is not in the right type of environment.* A value statement – values are different for everyone and so what the 'right' type of environment is would need to be made explicit and critically examined.

- *John has injuries.* An empirical statement – these injuries should be in evidence and are therefore verifiable. However, how and why they were sustained would need further detail to clearly establish any further implication here.

- *John is unhappy.* A conceptual statement – because concepts are ideas that relate to a class of objects, they are not specific. More detailed or empirical 'evidence' is needed to verify and make explicit what is meant precisely.

- *John will be subject to more abuse if we do not act.* A causal statement – assumes one thing affects another but the detail of the more specific connection and cause is missing.

# Establishing professional authority

Until recently, professional judgement and practical reasoning have perhaps not been given the full appreciation and value they deserve within social work practice and education. They may have been viewed as too tacit, practice-based or subjective, and inadvertently ignored in favour of a reliance on authority from external sources, e.g. theory or research, as justification for decisions and/or actions. Cameron (2009, p11) notes this *deeply embedded [knowledge] hierarchy inherent in the system*. It is hoped that professional judgement and practical reasoning can now become more explicit and examined as pivotal aspects of professional expertise. In our view it is sound practical reasoning that provides at least part of the necessary 'internal' authority and justification for establishing sound professional judgement. The principles detailed above in this chapter can be used as suitable evaluation criteria for CPD or PQ learning, encompassing as they do the necessary abilities for sound practical reasoning and deliberation with knowledge, skills and values in practical situations.

Indeed, it can be seen that practical reasoning underpins and informs professional deliberation and judgement across a wide range of dilemmas concerning what to do and how to it. So for John in our example above:

- from critically evaluating and interpreting a colleague's notes on John, or the latest theory on child development in respect of John's situation;

- to working out which piece of research is the most valid and appropriate for understanding John's behaviour;

- to considering the best way to communicate with John and his family;

- to deciding whether or not John needs to be removed from his family.

In the making of these decisions and their associated deliberations we can develop a robust ability to make sound judgements by making best critical use of our own expertise, as well as the expertise of others, in a clear and moral relationship with the situation at hand. It is this moral relationship between means and ends which is provided by practical reasoning. In becoming aware of this reasoning and deliberation as much as we can, and seeking to improve it, we are cultivating the judgement and authority which is at the heart of professional practice development.

# Review

This chapter has focused on some relevant aspects and processes of professional judgement, in particular practical reasoning, to show how critical thinking can help inform and enhance them. As professional judgement is at the heart of expertise and informs specific areas of practice such as decision-making and risk assessment, it is an area where critical consideration is crucial in establishing professional authority and in maintaining safe and accountable practice.

As we have seen, professional judgement and deliberation is applied to a wide range of deliberations and decisions in practice. The use of new knowledge in practice is one such key area and is the subject of the next chapter.

**Gray, M and Gibbons, J** (2007) There are no answers, only choices: Teaching ethical decision making in social work. *Australian Social Work*, 60 (2), 222–38.

This paper describes a learning unit that sought to teach students about ethical decision making as a critical thinking process.

**O'Sullivan, T** (2010) *Decision making in social work.* Second edition. London: Macmillan.

A new edition which provides a supportive framework for making social work judgements and assessments based on a structured and practical approach.

**Parsloe, P** (ed) (2010) *Risk assessment in social care and social work.* London: Jessica Kingsley.

This text outlines the theoretical issues behind the decisions, processes and organisations involved in risk assessment.

**Taylor, B** (2010) *Professional decision making in social work practice.* Exeter: Learning Matters.

Provides guidance and help for social work practitioners and students to make professional decisions with clients; from exercising statutory powers and duties to protect children from abuse, to making decisions about risk.

**Taylor, C and White, S** (2000) *Practising reflexivity in health and welfare. Making knowledge.* Buckingham: Open University Press.

This book explores how knowledge is used in professional practice and how it is constructed in everyday encounters.

# Chapter 4
## Using knowledge in practice

Post-qualifying learning will introduce you to a range of formal knowledge such as policy, legislation, theory and research in the specialist area of your choice. The Munro Review (Munro, 2011) highlights the importance of social workers' critical use of research evidence and theory to help them reach the most appropriate decisions.

We have seen in the previous chapter that professional judgement uses knowledge to help inform deliberations about what to do – practical reasoning activates and interprets a wide range of formal and informal knowledge, skills and values to this end. We can also see that the principles of practical reasoning help us undertake sound, moral reasoning and deliberation with knowledge in practical situations. In other words, we use knowledge when making professional judgements, but such use of knowledge involves professional judgement in its own right. This use of knowledge in practice will be an active and important learning experience because it cannot be applied systematically or predictably, and things won't necessarily go according to plan. It will be an interpretive process. Developing practice in this way, by putting into use new ideas and knowledge, is one of the most important ways critical thinking can be practised in the workplace (Argyris and Schön, 1974).

## Critical use of formal knowledge in practice

If we look at these processes more closely, we can see that formal knowledge (such as theory and research findings) can only inform practice; it cannot predict or control exactly what will take place. Theoretical methods, models and frameworks explaining the world we are in, what social work is and how to do it, as well as research evidence, can be extremely useful material for social workers (especially those who are newly qualified).

They help us gain more information and understanding about the issues as well as possible interventions and outcomes, but they cannot be taken 'off the shelf' as an unmediated solution. In fact, it would be difficult to reduce the complex, uncertain and unstable situations we work with to something that a standardised theoretical body of knowledge, or a set of specific research findings, can answer (Adams et al., 2002).

Initially new knowledge undergoes a process which aligns with the way we 'learn'. Learning is usually about fitting new material into existing material. It involves the processes of abstracting general principles from the new ideas so that they can be matched with, or connected to, the knowledge we already have (Sotto, 1994). Some of the original ideas, rules or procedures from this knowledge may remain relatively intact during this process, but the process itself produces new understanding. As Race (2001) puts it, the abstracting of principles or generalising involves a lot of 'digesting':

- sorting out what is important;

- extracting fundamental principles;

- discarding what is not important;

- establishing a sense of ownership of it.

For practical use, this knowledge will need to be interpreted and adapted further for the specific and unique conditions of any situation, and integrated with experience and values as well. In terms of practical reasoning this aligns with the situational appreciation and discernment necessary to ensure a moral and reasonable relationship between aims and outcomes. The justification for something being done or decided on is not made on the inherent authority of a theory or a piece of research (although their reliability and credibility is obviously important), but on the professional judgement (the reasoning, deliberation and decisions) that analysed and evaluated the information for a specific purpose.

There is no model or process for how formal knowledge is mediated to make it relevant and useful – such a transfer of knowledge is not an exact or linear process, but as practitioners we are constantly building on and using our inputs of information and knowledge whether we are fully aware of it or not. Mathews and Crawford's (2011) text provides an excellent guide to the critical use and development of knowledge in social work, supporting the view that an organic, evolving relationship between practice and knowledge is desirable.

ACTIVITY *4.1*

*Think about a particular theory you use a lot in practice – note the ways it has helped you understand a situation or decide what to do. Do you understand that theory differently now from when you first learnt about it? What are its strengths and its limitations?*

COMMENT

*Using theory proactively means interpreting it but also understanding how and why it is useful for each situation. This process will necessarily show up any limitations in the scope or depth of the theory, but you will probably understand the theory and your practice more by doing this. This is a creative process because you will be using your own experience and understanding, plus other formal or informal knowledge, to extend and adapt the theory as necessary as well.*

Using new knowledge gained from an academic environment for practice can at first be conscious and deliberative. There are a number of difficulties. As seen earlier, the authority of theories and research can be viewed as unchallengeable wisdom. To criticise this type of knowledge might seem presumptuous but it is important to show how knowledge meant for practice can be used for specific situations and how it actually 'performs' when used. By starting to use their judgement with this knowledge in particular cases with appropriate support and guidance (e.g. in supervision), newly qualified practitioners can develop their confidence, expertise and their own authority.

However, newly qualified practitioners may be more comfortable working with formal, external knowledge rather than more personal knowledge due to their lack of an established frame of reference built upon experience, and therefore confidence. Use of formal knowledge can then follow a deductive process, i.e. working from the generalised aspects of known theories and frameworks, or research findings, and mechanistically applying them to a particular situation. The issue here is that these ideas may be imposed on new situations in order to understand them, and the inherent meaning of the situation (usually contained within the detail) may be lost when trying to produce rational solutions. In effect, the situation may become manipulated to fit the template of the theory, which distorts true understanding. Instead, Margetson (2000, cited Nixon and Murr, 2006, p807) advocates an inductive approach, where reasoning is developed first from observed examples with reference back to formal knowledge. This enables more interpretive habits and develops a practitioner's professional judgement, confidence and authority, and, in turn, allows for the complexity of the situation to be taken into account. The inductive approach, therefore, creates a reinterpretation of meaning in new contexts rather than imposition of one truth across contexts. For Fook et al. (2000, p191) this becomes 'contextual theory development', which we can call the production of practice-based knowledge.

From a critical thinking perspective the process of using new knowledge in practice may require a framework to ensure certain activities are covered, which provides the process with a necessary robustness and validity. In other words we are trying to ensure that it is not merely a 'trial and error' exercise. Our framework for using new knowledge in practice (Table 4.1) is based on an inductive approach. It follows principles associated with practical reasoning and starts with an understanding of the practice situation. We have also aligned the process with useful evaluation and assessment criteria (QAAHE, 2008). Such a framework will help ensure that the process ultimately addresses situation-focused needs, but also allows you to demonstrate, evidence and evaluate the type of learning achieved.

**Table 4.1** Framework for using new knowledge in practice with associated assessment criteria

| Activities associated with using new knowledge in practice | General assessment criteria |
|---|---|
| A. Identify relevant general and/or specific aspects for the situation at hand | *Analysis, comprehension* |
| B. Judge this knowledge in respect of the situation's circumstances and needs, and its aims and objectives | *Critical appraisal, evaluation* |
| C. Combine principles with other knowledge, experience, ideas and values | *Transformation of abstract data and concepts, synthesis* |
| D. Use to inform or direct decisions and actions | *Design, creativity, transfer* |
| E. Critically monitor and judge new understanding and meaning | *Evaluation* |

Obviously, this process involves more than a straightforward or linear application of particular technical skills and is a highly reflective experience generating a practitioner's own knowledge for practice. Responsible assessment and deliberation will also be very apparent throughout the process, as well as other more implicit and less conscious elements, for example perception, interpretation, emotion, reflection. We will deal with the reflective element in a later chapter.

# Critical appraisal of formal knowledge

If we revisit our set of 'intellectual resources' for critical thinking we can see various alignments. Overall, the framework presented above can be seen to provide a number of critical thinking strategies.

---

*REFLECTION POINT*

*Where else in this framework (Table 4.1) would critical thinking intellectual resources be used and how?*

---

More specifically, critical thinking standards would be applied in activity B in Table 4.1, to allow a more general, critical appraisal of formal knowledge. These are detailed below.

## Standards for critical appraisal of theories (from Newman, c2000)

- According to this theory, what determines human behaviour?
- What are the major beliefs of the theory – which do I accept and why? Which don't I accept and why?
- Are the assumptions clearly defined; reasonable; ethically and socially consistent with my own and social work's assumptions and values?
- How applicable is the theory across settings, different clients and problems?
- Is the theory clear, easy to understand and logical?
- Does the theory address cultural, ethical or racial issues? Is it culturally sensitive?
- What is the empirical (testable) support for the theory?
- Is it original?
- How does the theory compare and contrast with other theoretical approaches?

## Standards for critical appraisal of research evidence

The critical appraisal of research evidence requires some specialist training, but these questions start you off.

- Have the authors clearly explained the purpose of the study, how it was carried out and the results?

- How confident can we be that the study sample is representative of the broader population – or does it relate to my clients?

- Did some people 'drop out' of the study, and if so have the authors accounted for this in their conclusions?

- Have the authors showed how the findings were 'worked out'?

- Have the authors any reason to be biased?

- Are the claims made by the study plausible?

- Does the study add anything to what we already know?

- The main question has to be: does it apply in my situation?

# Developing new understanding and practice-based knowledge

Lester (1995) has argued it is no longer adequate to base professional development on transmitting existing knowledge or developing a predefined range of competences. He wants practitioners to be able to construct and reconstruct the knowledge and skills they need and continually evolve their practice, in order to respond intelligently to unknown situations and go beyond established knowledge to create unique interpretations and outcomes. His ideas combine the notions of practical reasoning and professional judgement with the use and creation of practice-based knowledge. The expert 'skill' lies in being able to theorise the situation first in order to construct the problem to be solved. Key tools are analysis, synthesis, situational and ethical understandings, the ability to interpret the meanings of situations from a range of perspectives, as well as analytical and critical use of formal knowledge. What we have as a result is not a reduced concept of professional expertise but an appreciation of the divergent but also holistic, interconnected and value-based nature of situations and problems.

The creation of such professional knowledge from practice echoes earlier work by Schön (1983) and Eraut (1994), who advocate the support and guidance of practitioners through experience to understand and determine the value of this knowledge, and to critically evaluate the development of practice-based theories. A recent review (Nixon and Murr, 2006) of thinking in this area for social work practice has concluded that professional knowledge is created by a practitioner by combining and recombining more explicit theoretical knowledge with an understanding of tacit or implicit knowledge from professional processes. This legitimate generation of practice-based knowledge can take fuller account of the complexity and uncertainty of practice. In this respect, professional knowledge becomes more holistic and concerned with 'being' rather than just knowing, and thus necessarily complex and extensive.

ACTIVITY *4.2*

*Can you identify any practice-based knowledge you have created in this way and now work with?*

**COMMENT**

*As you start to articulate your ideas and ways of working you will probably recognise some of the different elements that make it up, e.g. your experience in seeing something work, your feelings and values, other people's ways of working, formal theories, research findings.*

We can also see that this practice-based knowledge, once legitimately generated and evaluated, can become potent material for PQ learning. The articulation of such knowledge within assignments and portfolios creates the necessary confidence and 'voice' from which to argue and reason more coherently and robustly. This is explored in more detail in Chapter 6. It also works towards a clearer understanding of a practitioner's or even a team's 'theories in use' (Argyris and Schön, 1974).

Although many practitioners see their practice-based knowledge as intuitive and personal and therefore unworthy of acknowledgement in an academic environment, it does not have to lack the rigour, testability or validity of academic knowledge if we can demonstrate critical awareness, validation and evaluation of it. Eraut (1994) in particular stated that professional education should not ignore the knowledge embedded in application and practice. Learning or developing practice knowledge can involve haphazard and unplanned processes. But practice is not always idiosyncratic, or necessarily implicit. Whatever is consciously and intentionally performed as practice implies an underpinning set of principles being acted upon. These principles will usually be based upon theoretical knowledge, experience, as well as values, and are at the heart of the notion of expertise. Argyris and Schön (1974); Schön (1983, 1987) and Eraut (1994) all develop the meaning of practice-based knowledge further.

The main point is that many of these principles can be explored and evidenced by identifying and appraising the processes and content of our reasoning and actions. In fact, to be totally unaware of them would be tantamount to not taking responsibility for the effects of our actions, which is unacceptable in any profession. As professional knowledge depends on the range of contexts in which it is used and tested, we can begin to create powerful meanings from our accumulated experience for the purposes of PQ learning. For many students the process of identifying, articulating and evaluating their practice-based knowledge has been a very empowering learning experience because they have begun to discover their own voice.

However, the articulation of developing practices may prove a challenge to those practitioners who have been out of formal education for a while. Trying to make our learning, experience and knowledge more explicit for PQ learning is a major undertaking. We need to take extra time to examine more closely what we do, why we do it and what this means. One way of dealing with this is to use reflection, which is the subject of the next chapter.

**Fisher, T and Somerton, J** ( 2000) Reflection on action: the process of helping social workers to develop their use of theory in practice. *Social Work Education,* 19 (4), 387–401.

This paper clarifies what integrating theory and practice actually means and also suggests a model for exploring the use of theory in practice for use in supervision.

**Mathews, I and Crawford, K** (2011) *Evidence-based practice in social work.* Exeter: Learning Matters.

A text that offers a critical approach to the debate concerning the reliability and validity of the evidence, research, and knowledge that underpins professional social work practice.

**Pawson, R, Boaz, A, Grayson, L, Long, A and Barnes, C** (2003) *Types and quality of knowledge in social care.* Knowledge Review No.3. London: SCIE.

This knowledge review identifies the main types of research, experience and wisdom that combine to form the social care knowledge base and proposes a framework for assessing the quality of knowledge of any type.

# Chapter 5
## Critical reflection

Critical thinking itself involves a reflective dimension and the idea of reflective learning is therefore closely connected to it (Brookfield, 1987). We may not always be sure about what reflection is (any more than we can fully understand what learning is) and Ixer (1999, 2010) in particular argues that we do not know enough about its processes to assess it validly. However, we can understand what it can do within our own context and we have already seen its place within practical reasoning and professional judgement.

The CPD Framework will encourage the articulation and assessment of learning and development occurring within educational and practice settings. Similarly, the Munro Review (Munro, 2011) describes the learning to be gained by engaging in deliberate practice built on reviewing prior experience to derive new insights and lessons, and on feedback that is accurate, diagnostic and timely. Reflection is therefore a central aspect to ongoing learning and development. Being reflective will allow awareness, analysis and evaluation of these educational and practice-based experiences in order to fully realise and better express the knowledge gained, and the learning and development that took place. The way you do this is a crucial factor in your achievement.

Emphasis is placed not on a descriptive account of what happened but on a full-scale examination of the hows, whys and 'what it all means' for future practice. In order to do this we would need to reflect deeply and critically upon the experience or situation.

## What is reflection?

When described in the literature critical reflection is usually referred to as the thinking activities engaged in to critically analyse and evaluate experiences, producing outcomes of new understandings and appreciations of the way we think and operate. The concept of self-awareness is always apparent within the associated concept of reflexivity, which allows the subjective element (feelings and emotions associated with a situation) to be analysed and evaluated at the same time. The consideration of external knowledge to provide a broad and current context may also be included.

Schön (1983, 1987) developed ideas around two main types of reflection for practice.

● 'Reflection on action' – when we think back on something already done.

● 'Reflection in action' – when we think about what we are doing while we are doing it.

Even though he uses the same term it would seem apparent that the processes are very different. When we are doing something we rarely have the time or opportunity to be consciously deliberative or analytical, and so the manner of our 'reflection' is likely to be much more holistic, intuitive and automatic in the latter situation (Van Manen, 1995).

For the former situation (reflection on action) we can think of reflection as a developing personal ability. Everyone seems to adopt their own method to help it happen: some people like to keep a journal, others make jottings or notes, some draw pictures or mind maps, and others just think in the bath. To do it effectively there are guidelines to follow, and deep and critical levels to achieve for PQ learning, and these will be explained below. All it takes is an ability to think, to be self-aware and to question – but it takes practice to develop a method suitable for you and attain the necessary level, as we don't always do this automatically. Practice needs time, commitment, and some support – these are the variables.

## What does it achieve?

Your reflection will produce a lot of thoughts, ideas, connections and insights into your learning and development. This also follows Schön's (1987) ideas, which explore how professional expertise is developed through the use of critical reflection. Rather than repeating the same experience or developing one's own implicit 'rules of thumb', etc., practitioners can explore, understand and justify their practice deliberations, decisions and actions in different ways using critical intellectual resources and develop new perspectives for future practice using available theory, research, knowledge and experience.

To use the earlier language of Argyris and Schön (1974), we reveal our 'theories-in-use' (the implicit theories that govern our actual behaviour and contain assumptions about self, others and environment) and examine them against our espoused theory (the words we use to convey what we do or what we would like others to think we do) to see if they fit. A small gap between the two might not be a bad thing but if it gets too wide then there is clearly a difficulty. Provided the two remain connected then the gap creates a dynamic for reflection and for dialogue.

However, our need goes beyond being a reflective practitioner in a narrow sense. Because reflection for our purposes is in a social work education context, the main outcome of reflection is seen to be an identification and evaluation of the learning and development pertaining to future practice, i.e. the development of the self as a critical practitioner (Adams et al, 2002). The aim is to think beyond the acknowledgement and description of difficult aspects of a situation to an evaluation of how they were dealt with, i.e. the resulting action, as well as its meaning and significance.

The overall standards of learning in this context therefore concern change and development. These ideas are discussed in more depth by Mezirow et al. (1990) as the development of practice to oppose and redress power imbalances. The main outcome of critical reflection on practice in a social work context will therefore be an identification and evaluation of that learning and development relevant to values, as well as future practice methods.

Argyris and Schön (1974) call it 'double-loop learning' when an 'error' is detected and corrected in ways that involve the modification of underlying norms, values and objectives, as well as the techniques or strategies. In other words we need to not only ask if we are doing things right, but also if we are doing the right thing and how do we decide what is right. They argue that double-loop learning is necessary if practitioners are to make informed decisions in rapidly changing and often uncertain contexts. This learning should also encompass and, if possible, inform policy changes at organisational level where appropriate.

# How far do we go with reflection?

Kolb (1984), using earlier work by others including Rogers, Piaget and Lewin, further developed a model called the experiential learning cycle, where the learner changes from an active participant in an experience, to a reflector on it, to an analyst of it, and then onto an experimenter with new ideas for a new experience. Reflective learning for us goes further to draw out the complete 'learning' for the person and their practice from the experiential process, and links the critical incidents to ideas and theories which shed light on them (Beatty, 2003, cited in Parker, 2004). So being 'reflective' means exploring experiences (positive and negative; small or large) and moving into new understanding. New understanding is key feature of a deep approach to learning, as opposed to surface learning or memorising.

Reflective processes can guide our learning experiences during an event and they can also guide our ability to express or show how this change occurred after the event (Moon, 2001). Academic assignments might ask you to explore your 'reflections' or thoughts before, during and after an experience. As we have already discussed, 'reflection in action' is much more intuitive and so will be harder to articulate later on. Taking the time and space to take a step back from an event, or adopting a 'helicopter view' over it, may help you. Many students have said how reading up on a practice area also helps them clarify their thoughts.

The rule is that academic reflection usually has to show knowledge, critical thought, analysis, evaluation and output. Deeper levels of reflection will therefore gain more marks than shallow ones and we will now explore them in detail.

# Levels of reflection

There are a number of models of reflection that can be followed to develop deeper levels and your choice will be a personal one. There are certain aspects common to most of these models and they have been collated and simplified in Table 5.1 in a framework, again with the associated general assessment criteria (QAAHE, 2008).

**Table 5.1** Framework of reflective levels with associated assessment criteria

| Key levels and aspects of reflection | General assessment criteria |
|---|---|
| **Description**<br>Show a full awareness of self and the situation/experience,<br>i.e. What, who, when, where...? | *Identification, definition* |
| **Critical analysis**<br>Identify and explore significant aspects and issues of this situation, e.g. feelings, behaviour, actions, decisions, etc.<br>Challenge or question underlying assumptions, knowledge, experience, etc.,<br>i.e. How, why...? | *Analysis, critical appraisal* |
| **Evaluation**<br>Judge input, deliberations, decisions and outcomes; include ideas, information, knowledge, experience, values, professional powers, risk.<br>Show additional insight into relevant issues; wider contexts; different perspectives,<br>i.e. How well...? What about...? | *Evaluation, judgement*<br><br>*Insight, synthesis, creativity* |
| **Learning**<br>Produce and evaluate new understandings, perspectives, creative/ original solutions, development, change or learning for practice methods and values,<br>i.e. What does this mean...? | *Development of self and practice knowledge*<br>*Personal responsibility*<br>*Professional competencies and capabilities* |

Of course it is not possible to regard these levels as totally distinct or mutually exclusive from each other and, as seen before, there are many other more implicit elements not included. However, we can revisit our intellectual resources for critical thinking and note various applications throughout.

---

*QUESTION*

*Where do you think critical thinking intellectual resources (seen in Chapter 2) should be used within these levels and how?*

---

In order to understand how the levels interrelate and lead on from one another we will look at an analogy – school science lessons. The way they were written up usually followed a format like the following.

---

### *Example*
**Reflection on a science lesson**

*The order for the write-up*

- *Apparatus*: What did we use? Test tube, Bunsen burner, chemicals.
- *Method*: What did we do? The chemicals were heated in the test tube over the Bunsen burner.
- *Results*: What happened? It went bang!
- *Conclusion:* Why did that happen? The flame was too high.

The apparatus, methods and results sections can be seen to echo the first level of reflection (description), i.e. they are a mere reporting of the facts about what was done and what happened. The experiment's conclusion, an investigation of why the result happened as it did, echoes the second stage of reflection (analysis). This 'uncovering' process would show the teacher how much understanding occurred. For example: did the pupils realise the chemicals reacted differently at different temperatures, etc.?

So this is where the reasons, the issues and factors, behind what has happened are thought about in detail, and therefore hopefully uncovered, analysed and explained. It is easy to confuse the reporting of results with an understanding of conclusions. The observational process is important but understanding why something happened, rather than just knowing what happened, is an important stage in learning. However, deeper learning goes beyond this and involves further reflection and investigation.

The next level of reflection (evaluation) can only happen when the previous stage has taken place. In our example we know the flame was too high and this caused the chemicals to explode but we need to know whether an explosion was our original aim or required outcome. If we did not want an explosion to happen, the outcome is deemed to be 'wrong' and we would want to make sure it didn't happen again. We therefore need to know why the flame was too high on the Bunsen burner. Further investigation might show that the flame regulator on the burner got stuck and couldn't be altered at the crucial moment. By looking deeper and enhancing our understanding of the situation we not only know how well we did, we also have new issues to reflect on. We can now use this new information to move onto the final stage.

The last level of reflection (learning) takes us into an area of thinking about the future and into action, i.e. what has been learnt, what does this mean, what changes are needed? In our classroom situation we might think that because the chemicals needed a low temperature it would be important to check the equipment before use next time. This new understanding and learning would not have occurred without deeper reflection and evaluation of the original outcome.

---

Obviously this is a very simple analogy which does not include important aspects of self, context and values, but it shows how deeper and more critical reflection creates greater understanding and further learning.

---

*ACTIVITY* **5.1**

*Write out one of your own practice experiences using these levels, but try to include some of the aspects we missed – i.e. feelings/self; the wider context; values.*

**COMMENT**

*Delving deeper into what was happening etc., can help you uncover the more significant and relevant (but less obvious) aspects that may have been missed or unconsciously passed over. It can also help to understand the part you played and the wider context too.*

---

Reflection on some experiences may go even further and change deep and personally held beliefs, assumptions or inner values. If this happens you may need the extra support of someone you trust to help you deal with it, so it is important you recognise this as soon as it starts to happen.

# Can it end up a bit negative?

It can feel negative when things we try in practice don't turn out the way we expect. We can start to feel anxious and defensive when having to think about it all again. But we are dealing with real life and your supervisor or tutors will actually expect a conflict between prior expectations and experiences. What is required is that this conflict is not ignored or glossed over but explored further in order to develop practice. What is certain is that 'false accounts' of reflection are fairly easy to spot. If you are at all unsure about how much or what you are supposed to 'reveal' then ask your tutors to be as explicit as possible regarding what they are looking for. They should distinguish between what is deemed 'public information', and thus used for assessment, and what is personal and private.

Understanding new ideas can involve the reassessment of old perspectives, which can be discomforting, whereas exploring the things that have gone right can affirm and help understanding of experience and knowledge in more detail. But reflecting on all types of experiences (the negative and positive) can:

• allow greater awareness and expression of all types of learning and development;

• show enhanced understanding from why things did work, as well as why they didn't;

• provide a more positive ending for the negative experiences rather than just leaving things as they were, and allow a proper and full recognition of the good experiences and one's strengths.

We also need to understand how to apply or transfer these strengths and work with our talents in new or more difficult situations. We already possess much of what we need to develop but a lot of it lies hidden or unrecognised unless it is reflected on. Reflection on problems can weaken confidence to develop in self-reflective ways (Weick et al., 1989) but a shift towards possibilities creates new, positive and individual paths for people. This is a 'strengths-perspective' approach for enabling others. Learning to transfer strengths from one setting to another is a key component in lifelong learning.

However, placing oneself at the centre of an event or experience can lead to a preoccupation with the self that can border on self-absorption. To avoid this happening, ensure that your reflection turns outwards as well, i.e. onto practice values, principles, traditions and the wider context relevant to the issue. Also be aware that reflection is not foolproof. Remembering the past is dependent on many different factors and is fallible. When an experience is reflected on, the original event becomes shaped and coloured by that reflection. Many courses advise the keeping of notes or a journal of some sort to record and preserve what actually happened and enable more accurate recall at a later date.

Other useful activities to develop reflection are questioning and sharing thoughts with others, which is why group work and communication with colleagues and fellow students is particularly important for PQ learning and most CPD situations.

# Review

Reflecting deeply and critically is about making sure that all the aspects above are covered – i.e. there is an evaluated outcome or conclusion in terms of your understanding and learning and development. These ideas provide the necessary elements to write about in PQ work but it is important to understand academic writing style in order to articulate ideas in the correct way when in a formal learning environment. The following chapter will elaborate on this.

*FURTHER READING*

**Rolfe, G, Freshwater, D and Jasper, M** (2001) *Critical reflection for nursing and the helping professions.* London: Palgrave.

This practical user's guide offers a range of clear frameworks and structures of reflective practice, including individual and group supervision, reflective writing and research.

**Thompson, S and Thompson, N** (2008) *The critically reflective practitioner.* London: Palgrave Macmillan.

This is essential reading for making sense of reflective practice, looking at what it is, what it is not, and what it can be at its best.

# Chapter 6

# Writing reflective academic assignments

**ACHIEVING POST QUALIFYING SOCIAL WORK AWARDS**

This chapter will help you to meet the following National Occupational Standards for Social Work.
*Key role 6: Unit 18: Research, analyse, evaluate and use current knowledge of best social work practice*
*Key role 6: Unit 19: Work within agreed standards of social work practice and ensure own professional development*
If you are a registered social worker, this chapter will also assist you to evidence these areas of the Professional Capabilities Framework:
• Knowledge
• Professionalism.

This section focuses on reflective academic assignments which aim to integrate theory and practice and articulate professional judgement, and suggests ways to structure and write them using the guidelines we give our own students. Not all universities adopt this style of assignment for PQ learning, and different institutions will assess reflective assignments in various ways for each of the academic levels, so it is necessary to check with your tutors before you follow the guidance given here. However, this guidance is based on years of teaching experience and of external assessment, so we feel confident of its value.

In general, the reflective assignment needs to show and evidence the understanding and use of academic knowledge, the learning outcomes achieved and professional development. It is therefore not a description of events or feelings. It should allow your learning derived from your critical thinking and reflection to be expressed.

How you view any assignment will depend on your previous experiences of education and the length of time since being a formal 'learner', but it will be important not to make any assumptions and to follow your course handbooks and assignment guidelines very carefully.

## Benefits of writing

Academic assessment can be dominated by written work. As with most qualifications it is not what you think or do, but the way you articulate it that is graded. Assignment writing is therefore important because it is a major way in which existing or developing practice can be expressed for assessment purposes. This is a positive aspect because we understand and learn more while we are writing as the process supports and develops reflective and critical abilities. It is also a skill social workers must acquire as it is often via written reports that clients are represented. This cannot be overstated. Good social work often requires the writing of reports for the benefit of the client and well-written reports will require the same skills.

According to Moon (1999a), writing:

- forces us to spend the time;

- helps us focus and sift material by slowing us down;

- forces us to organise and clarify our thoughts so we can sequence them;

- gives us a structure;

- gives control – we choose which points to make – enables identification and prioritising of material;

- helps us to know if we do understand something by attempting to explain it;

- can help develop a deeper understanding of something as we work through it and explain it;

- can record a train of thought and relate it to the past, present and future;

- can initiate new ideas, connections, questions, etc.

Because critical reflection relies so much on making connections and judging our thoughts and information, writing is one of the main activities that can help by starting this process of capturing and expressing basic assumptions, underlying knowledge and the memory of any experience. Writing skills are primarily thinking skills but because writing is slower it can achieve more, especially in developing connections, exploring the experience more deeply, and gaining different perspectives.

Writing is not a one-off activity. All writing is about drafting and rewriting. It has a powerful effect in prompting further insights and hunches – the problem is that once we write these down they sound clumsy. This is because these ideas come into our minds as holistic and compacted 'nuggets', if you like. To convey them in structured language is like trying to translate them from one code into another. It won't happen in one or two attempts, unfortunately. Also, this translation process will throw up further ideas as we explore and unravel the original one. It is no wonder we go off on tangents and get lost. The key is to have a structure and a disciplined approach so that we can work with and control all these thoughts and articulate a clear message from them.

We wish to point out here that we believe PQ assignments need to be based on, and reflect, your practice – hence critical reflection. Society does not need social workers who can write theoretically about practice but cannot practice competently or reflect on their own practice; society needs capable, skilled practitioners. In other words, society needs social workers who can critically reflect on their practice and debate and demonstrate competence and capability articulately.

# Coverage

Choosing what to write about will obviously depend entirely on what the assignment is for but it will usually be concerned with new knowledge becoming embedded in practice. A study of the assignment content guidelines and learning outcomes will identify all the areas to cover. Then you can decide which experiences or examples will be able to show and evidence these areas best; or plan for a new experience to allow this. List the areas the assignment wants you to cover. Then develop some ideas around them. How you do this is up to you; everyone has a different way, whether it's using lists or pictures. But do start – even if it's with 'Once a upon a time...'. Only when something is down on paper or on a PC can you begin to work on it and make it better – if it's stuck in your head it's probably just going to float about doing nothing except worry you.

# Using the reflective levels

As we have seen, reflecting in the PQ context is about concentrating on the deeper, critical levels, i.e. to ensure that there is an outcome in terms of your understanding, evaluation and learning about the education and practice events you are involved with – your professional development. If we re-examine the reflective levels, we can see that the questions associated with each of them can also help develop our initial, often more descriptive, thoughts and reflections onto more analytical and evaluative levels. See Table 6.1.

**Table 6.1** Questions to develop descriptive reflection towards learning

| Description | Critical analysis | Evaluation | Learning |
|---|---|---|---|
| What did you do? What happened? What did you feel? | How did you do it? Why did you do it that way and not a different way? What was important and significant – why? | How far and in what ways were your goals met? What other factors were apparent? | So what does this mean for future practice and your values? |

We can go further and identify the type of material that might need to be included in answers to these questions at each level. See Table 6.2.

**Table 6.2** Type of material to include at each reflective level

| Description | Critical analysis | Evaluation | Learning |
|---|---|---|---|
| Background | Theory, research, policy, legislation | Judgement, measurement of progress and outcome/s | Abstracting general principles |
| Context | Experience, practice knowledge | Strengths, weaknesses, gaps | Insights, ideas, new perspectives |

| Feelings | Values, ethics, conflicts | Counter-arguments and theories | Synthesis with existing knowledge |
|---|---|---|---|
| Specific relevant details | Aims and objectives | Wider context, other factors | Professional development |
| Definitions | Judgements, assumptions | Different perspectives | Future planning, changes |
| | Decisions, deliberations; reflection 'before, in and after action' | Alternatives | Further theory, research |

Table 6.2 mainly follows a 'reflection-on-action' idea (Schön, 1983) and a linear progression from left to right. It is not meant to be a prescriptive approach and you can use it in any way that helps. However, there is much this table cannot account for – i.e. the subtlety, depth, emotion and intuition involved in learning and thinking. Some of the questions or areas may not be relevant to your experience or reflection, and your own individual style and approach may require more holistic guidance to follow.

We are merely suggesting that reflective writing is a developmental and ongoing process, requiring time and feedback, and the elements noted above are all important aspects to be included because they are the elements usually being assessed for the PQ awards. At its heart PQ learning is about the demonstration of competence and capability to practise and this cannot occur without reflection on your practice.

# Structure – developing an 'argument'

## Stage 1: Developing a viewpoint and starting to make an argument

The starting point for structuring an assignment of this type is your overall point of view, your central idea, or your basic 'claim'. You cannot really start writing a first complete draft until you know what it is you want to say. And you won't know this until all the stages of the reflection process, and initial reading of the subject area, have been achieved. Your viewpoint consists of what has been understood and learnt, plus what this means for your practice and values. A viewpoint forms the basis of your overall 'argument' and allows you to control the material and develop your own voice. This does not mean that the assignment has to formally argue for or against something. It simply means that there has to be a coherent thread or series of connected points running through it, pursuing an idea and/ or the implications of an issue in practice. If you get stuck at this stage use Table 6.1, which may help you to reflect more deeply. If you still feel lost, try discussing with a tutor or supervisor. Even the smallest practice incidents can be packed with implicit new knowledge or learning but you may not be able see it for yourself without some critical questioning.

Developing the confidence to work with material in a way that allows your unique interpretation to be valued is a key underpinning aspect of academic, PQ and CPD learning. As we have seen, recent literature concerning professional knowledge in social work emphasises the legitimate generation of practice-based knowledge, where practice expertise is integrated with formal knowledge, and which is able to take full account of the complexity and uncertainty of practice (e.g. Fook et al., 2000; Mathews and Crawford, 2011).

The following is a simplified example of a viewpoint.

---

### Example
**Assignment for a specialist area of social work: enabling others**

**Stage 1: My viewpoint or the central idea**

'Good communication is essential when planning successfully for a placement student.'

Notes – I have learnt that because we need people in order to achieve things, communicating effectively with them helps us achieve more. This is another way we can show respect to others. The literature on placement planning generally agrees. Some authors do not give this area a lot of emphasis, though.

---

## Stage 2: Reasons give the structure a sequence

Once your viewpoint is known, you can then focus any further reflection and research on the pivotal themes and issues that form and establish this point of view, i.e. the reasons that support it. These can consist of formal and informal knowledge and evidence at this stage. For a 5,000-word assignment you will probably only be able to focus effectively on three or four main reasons. Too often we pick a subject that is just too big. Focus down – this will give you space to be analytical and not descriptive. These reasons should be organised in a way that can best persuade your reader to agree.

By expressing your viewpoint and reasons/themes in this way, you are making a claim, and the next stage is to sustain this claim in response to (or in anticipation of) a 'challenge' when you are in an academic environment. In other words, you now have to show the validity of this view and your commitment to it. This is not unusual, unique or inappropriate – social workers are constantly justifying their decisions and actions when challenged by service users, or managers, or colleagues in practice.

We can refer back to our viewpoint example and show some reasons for it.

---

### Example
**Assignment for a specialist area of social work: enabling others**

Stage 1: My viewpoint

'Good communication is essential when planning successfully for a placement student.'

Stage 2: The reasons why I believe good communication is essential

---

1. Interpersonal skills (good listening) helped me start the relationship with the student well – empathy, trust being built. Literature on interpersonal communication says these skills are crucial in forming relationships and for education. Dangers to be aware of are becoming too informal and friendly...

2. Better forming of communication lines with the university tutor would have enabled better understanding of their role and the ways I needed to liaise with them. I felt intimidated, and assumed the tutor would not be available; bureaucracy issues were apparent. Literature on placements says this is a difficult area – need to be proactive. I can discuss ways I could do this better next time...

3. Liaison with my team beforehand helped the induction go smoothly – people on side, better prepared. Literature about team co-ordination says that early contact allows problems to surface and be dealt before start. Literature on placement planning says early contact is essential but to also keep overall control by forming clear learning objectives for the student.

*ACTIVITY* **6.1**

*If such a structure is useful to you, start to develop one for an assignment of your own. Our example was very linear in structure but you can do it using any method you like.*

**COMMENT**

*Understanding and deciding what your main viewpoint is may take some time and may also change as you start writing and/or read more material. This is usual as it is a learning process but it means you need to continue to reflect and also focus. Revisit any assignment guidance and intended learning outcomes to make sure you are covering relevant topics etc. and not going off track.*

## Stage 3: Developing points for each reason will make up the paragraphs

Under each of your reasons develop a series of smaller but key points, using paragraphs, to show how and why they are relevant, etc., using evidence from theory/research/policy/legislation/experience/values to discuss/debate/challenge ideas presented. Each reason or theme will then need its own 'conclusion' which links back to the main argument/point of view.

By showing where evidence has come from (by citing and referencing it), or showing how it has been formed as a robust process, you can demonstrate its authority, reliability and validity for this purpose; in other words, apply relevant critical standards to it. Also look for material that contradicts your opinions to show that you are aware of, and have considered, arguments that are counter to your own. This will help clarify and sharpen your own ideas and help you demonstrate why they are more convincing. Their use is a good guiding critical principle. We have already shown in Chapter 4 how you can use the literature in practice more directly by critically examining how and why you adapted an idea for your own use, i.e. evaluate its purpose and usefulness for a situation.

To achieve an appropriate academic style you must view all knowledge as contextual (Baxter Magolda, 1992), i.e. there are no completely right or wrong answers out there but the knowledge or evidence supporting opinions and views can constructed, understood and appraised in relation to a particular context or situation. As we have said, there is no absolute 'truth' and your tutor will be assessing your ability to gain an overview of the subject and support a particular position within it.

# Paragraphs and signposting

Remember the idea is to try to persuade the reader. Often the first sentence is the key point itself – i.e. it explains what the paragraph is about and contains the main idea. This 'topic sentence' need not come first in the paragraph but it has to be somewhere because it asserts and controls the paragraph's main idea. You can place it in the middle if you have information that needs to precede it. You can put it at the end if you want to your reader to consider your line of reasoning before you declare your main point.

However you do it, the line of reasoning and its evidence should be linked logically within these paragraphs. As you develop the point you tell the reader where you are going with it, by making use of the literature, linking back to the reason and the main argument as appropriate. Ideally it is best to sort out one point before moving onto another, but if you do need to stop and then return to a point later, make sure you tell the reader what you're doing and why.

The next point should always be introduced. Using linking words or 'signposts' helps the reader make the transition from one paragraph or point to the next. There are different ways to do this depending on the way you want to develop your argument.

Here are some examples.

- Contrast, or taking a sudden turn in reasoning – 'but…', 'however…', 'on the other hand…', 'although…', 'and yet…'

- Cause and effect – 'therefore…', 'as a result of…', 'for this reason…', 'consequently…'

- Sequence – 'following…', 'before…', 'first…', finally…'

- Illustration – 'for example…', 'for instance…', 'such as…', 'in this case…'

- Add weight – 'similarly…', 'in addition…', 'moreover…'

- Conclusion – 'in conclusion…', 'accordingly…', 'to sum up…'

Returning to our example we can see a specific point being developed for the first reason.

> ### *Example*
> **Assignment for a specialist area of social work: enabling others**
>
> Stage 1: My viewpoint:
>
> 'Good communication is essential when planning successfully for a placement student.'
>
> Stage 2: First reason:
>
> 1. 'Interpersonal skills (good listening) helped me start the relationship with the student well – empathy, trust being built.'
>
> Stage 3: Particular point/issue to develop for this reason:
>
> **This is the point (topic sentence)** – Listening to the student rather than talking at her made our initial meeting a very positive one.
>
> **Define** – 'Listening entails....'
>
> **Develop – how and why** – 'Letting the student speak first not only allowed me an understanding of her unique situation and needs, it also made her feel at ease with me and to start to trust me...'
>
> **Link to reason/argument** – 'Understanding her needs and circumstances informed my planning...; but this conversation also formed a bond between us...'
>
> **Evidence/connections** – 'Bloggs (2003) explains how listening is more important than talking because it shows respect to others...and she responded by...' 'Adult learning theory similarly emphasises the need for respect for learners...'
>
> **Link to next point/paragraph** – 'However, the relationship still needs to remain professional...'

Once your main text is structured you will need an introduction and a conclusion.

# Introduction

We want to emphasise the crucial importance of the introduction. This is probably the most important part of your work in terms of ensuring your writing keeps to task. Don't attempt it until you have a good grip on your argument, reasons and points.

- Set the overall context but also state the main issues you are going to write and why, it will help you focus and places your 'argument' into a wider picture.

- Point out the limitations and what you are not going to consider.

- Introduce the structure and sequence of your work.

# Conclusion

A conclusion is all too often just a paragraph stuck on the end of the piece of work, which either summarises what has come before or gives the result of what happened.

A conclusion offers the chance to do much more than this. It can deliver a concise consideration of the overall meaning you have gained from critical thinking and reflection on your practice and/or learning. That is, it can sum up the major issues and points raised from your evaluation of the outcomes and consequences, plus what they may, or will mean for social work, for your practice or for yourself.

---

*ACTIVITY* **6.2**

*Try writing a brief introduction or conclusion for our example assignment.*

**COMMENT**

*It is useful if the introduction (and the conclusion) provides some linking phrases to tell the reader where you are going (or what you have shown) with your ideas. For example an introduction could say: This assignment will look initially at... to show that...;... followed by an examination of... to demonstrate that...;... whilst exploring issues around... to understand how...*

---

# Critical style

Developing an appropriate critical style does take time and practice, especially when initial thoughts tend to be very descriptive – here are some more tips. Table 6.3 shows how the more normal, descriptive way of writing can be developed into a critical academic style by listing how each element should be enhanced. Again we can see similar methods of questioning, delving deeper, assessing and judging things as we do in critical thinking abilities.

**Table 6.3** Descriptive to critical writing (Cottrell, 2003, p232)

| Descriptive writing | Critical analytical writing |
|---|---|
| States what happened | Identifies the significance |
| States what something is like | Evaluates (judges the value of) strengths and weaknesses |
| Gives the story so far | Weighs one piece of information against another |
| States the order in which things happened | Makes reasoned judgements |
| Says how to do something | Argues a case according to the evidence |
| Explains what a theory says | Shows why something is relevant or suitable |
| Explains how something works | Indicates why something will work (best) |
| Notes the method used | Indicates whether something is appropriate or suitable |

| Says when something occurred | Identifies why the timing is of importance |
|---|---|
| States the different components | Weighs up the importance of component parts |
| States options | Gives reasons for selecting each option |
| Lists details | Evaluates the relative significance of details |
| Lists in any order | Structures information in order of importance |
| States links between items | Shows the relevance of links between pieces of info |
| Gives information | Draws conclusions |

# Academic style – some hints for vocabulary and grammar

Try more formal, specific words, e.g.:

- 'examine' instead of 'look at';
- 'has the potential' instead of 'might';
- 'enables' instead of 'makes it possible'.

Try the passive voice in places:

- 'Assessments are started by gathering relevant information' instead of 'you start assessments by gathering relevant information'.

Use more cautious language to avoid sweeping statements:

- 'The introduction of the new policy could be seen as...'

Use noun phrases which cut down the use of words, especially verbs for a more succinct text:

- 'Carer's rights' instead of 'The rights of the carer';
- 'Recently issued policies' instead of 'Policies that have been issued recently';
- 'The effectiveness of the courses made them very popular' instead of 'The treatments were effective and this made them very popular'.

# Using the literature

As you probably realise, your success very much depends on the type of literature you read (its relevancy and authority) and your understanding of it, not how much you read. Quality not quantity! As a practitioner you will also be using contextual information such as legislation, case law, policy, and practice guidance documents, as well as theory and research. Your tutor, your reading lists and handouts will direct you to relevant and authoritative literature and you will be looking up more references for any specialist areas, using print and electronic resources. The particular problem areas associated with using literature are detailed below.

## Making unsubstantiated comments

One of the biggest single pieces of advice given back to students is: 'Do not make unsubstantiated comments, or sweeping generalisations'. Be clear about the difference between making points regarding your own practice and about social work practice in general. Evidence from your own practice experiences should be discussed as evaluated reflective practice rather than as mere anecdotes. Formal knowledge will help critically discuss the points you are making, but it is important to know how far it is expected to 'back you up' and whether you are allowed to discuss your expertise in a way that also evidences its own authority rather than relying entirely on the authority of others. Any generalised assertions, ideas and opinions made about social work in a broader sense, though, do require evidence from external, formal sources (in the form of references to previous writers, policies, legislation, etc.) to firmly support them.

We believe that in order to effectively develop their expertise, PQ learners in particular should not be expected to rely entirely on the ideas or authority of others in relation to their practice. They need to be able to discuss their development of practice and practice-based knowledge in a way that evidences its own authority (e.g. via sound practical reasoning, judgement or decision-making), as well as using formal knowledge to help critically inform, explain or explore the points being made.

## Avoiding plagiarism

You need to say where any evidence or ideas which are not your own have come from, otherwise you will be making claims to research/ideas/etc. that is not yours (which is plagiarism). Therefore references to evidence in the literature should appear whenever you are mentioning another's ideas, theory, material or research, whether you are directly quoting or paraphrasing them. This has to follow certain academic 'rules' in order to be valid and you should follow the appropriate system as advocated by your academic institution.

You can use someone else's work in three main ways.

1  You can mention their theory or idea:

   *The process used incorporated some of the elements of task-centred work (Coulshed, 1991) and systems approach (Payne, 1991; Milner and O'Byrne, 1998) because the...*

2  You can summarise in your own words what someone else has written, either small sections or overall views:

   *Mrs Jones felt helpless and frustrated at her inability to improve her daughter's situation and appeared to get many colds and coughs during this time which weakened her ability to look after her. Research has shown that those who experience life events that are seen as uncontrollable are more likely to become ill (Stern et al., 2003, cited in Gross, 2004).*

3 You can repeat a small section of what someone has written and place it in quotation marks, or indent it:

> *It is not sufficient to be reflective; we also need to use new understandings in our future actions. As Adams et al. (2002, p87) point out: 'reflection on its own views the situation unchanged, whereas critical practice is capable of change'.*

When paraphrasing:

- express the person's main ideas in your own words;

- keep it simple and concise;

- don't use the same sentence structure.

Try this method of remembering how to present other people's evidence: Ask – 'says who?' and 'so what?'. In other words, say who says this – the idea and the reference to who said it, and then state why you are telling the reader this – what is your point here? Often we read assignments and case studies and ask ourselves what is the point of the writer telling us that because it just appears to be packaging. Always ask yourself: what am I trying to say and why is it important? It will help you to be more focused.

If you use quotes then 'pick out' the key words and extend the discussion with them and the ideas being presented, e.g.:

> *Smith (2002, p.55) advocates that, 'it is very important that everyone involved in a process of improving service quality has a shared understanding of the issues and what is expected of them'. Sharing and understanding expectations are therefore key aspects to bear in mind when communicating with colleagues... however...*

Or paraphrase, and then lead into the discussion and start to support the point being made:

> *It is essential that expectations are shared and understood by everyone involved in situations concerning service improvement (Smith, 2002). Communication strategies are therefore of major importance... however...*

or

> *A key aim with service quality development is clear communication and an exchange of information and ideas for staff, especially about roles and the type of activities they would be involved with. As Smith (2002) shows, it is essential that expectations are shared and understood in such situations. However...*

Whichever way you use the work of other people, you must cite where the work came from in the text itself and provide a reference to the complete work in either a references list or a bibliography at the end of your work. In the Harvard system of referencing the citation in the text uses the author's last name and year, and the references list or bibliography will be in alphabetical order by author's last name. It is important to look up the rules for your particular institution and become familiar with them. See Appendix 1 for further help on the Harvard style of referencing (which is slightly different to the style used in this book).

## Effective reading

It does take time and practice to develop your reading in order to locate relevant and useful material. Here are a few initial ideas to help you start.

- Use any guidance provided by an educational institution or training department on gaining access to and using the most relevant electronic databases and printed materials. Use librarians for advice too. You don't want to waste time at this end of the process.

- Reading the literature while you are developing your viewpoint should encompass the wider topic area. Reading when you know your viewpoint will enable you to focus and identify the more relevant pieces of text easily and save your time. Make a note of particular quotes (keep them as short as possible) or paraphrase ideas (summarise in your own words). Also note the complete reference to the book, journal etc., at the time.

- Next, write down a brief explanation of what this means to you – what do you understand it to mean – do you agree or disagree with it – why? This becomes easier if you are applying what you read into practice straight away, or you have opportunities for discussion about the literature with your peers.

- As we have seen, as you start writing the first draft of your assignment you will have a good idea of what you are trying to say, so when you refer back to these notes you can choose those that are applicable to what you are talking about and integrate them.

## Using the first person 'I'

N.B. You must check your institution's own rules on this – some universities do not allow the use of the first person in written assignments.

Using the first-person 'I' is appropriate for academic reflective writing and for developing personal and professional qualities of self-awareness, reflection, analysis and critique (Hamill, 1999). However, this does not mean the writing should be emotional or subjective (i.e. seen from your viewpoint only). Students who lack experience in writing and who start to use 'I' tend to be too descriptive in their style – e.g. 'I did this...' 'I did that...'. So 'I' has to be used carefully and much care has to be taken to avoid informal or conversational tones within a reflective assignment. Using 'I' should encourage a confident stance, i.e. directness in saying what you mean and the message you are trying to get across. With the addition of the literature, and your viewpoint and reasons, it creates an appropriate academic style.

Here is a short general example from social work to show how it can all come together (from Watson et al., 2002, p128).

> *I would argue that it is how we as social workers use our legal power in practice that is the crux of developing partnership. That we have legal power does not absolve us of our professional duty to our clients. Jenny and her family members had a right to be treated with respect, openness and honesty (Banks, 1995) in my interventions with them. To me, this included acknowledging to them the impact on their lives that my legal power to intervene to safeguard and promote Jenny's welfare was having.*

*Research indicates that family members stressed the importance of being cared about as people (Thoburn, Lewis and Shemmings, 1995). This extended to identifying and acknowledging areas of Mr. Jones's care where he was safeguarding and promoting Jenny's welfare. As Morrison (1996, p136) suggests, 'Partnership is about working with parents and their networks to enable them to carry out the responsibility shared by both the state and parents to promote the welfare of children.'*

# Finishing writing

Check coverage and relevancy – match what you say you will focus on in the introduction against what you have written about in the main body and the conclusion. Also, refer back to your original list of what the assignment has to cover – make sure you have covered all that is asked of you. Ask yourself – 'where have I shown this?'

Think critically about your work before handing it in. Evaluate it using the guidance given here or even try marking it using your institution's assessment criteria.

# Review

As we have seen, writing is a process. Each draft will enable you to show areas of learning and development in more structured, explicit and academic ways as you build up a better understanding of what you have done. The main difficulty with writing is to get the real meaning of what you are trying to say past the code of language in which you have to say it.

Each rewrite should allow this by giving you the opportunity to:

- think about and analyse what you want to say more thoroughly;

- reflect on what you have achieved or learnt more deeply;

- read more around the issues and increase your ability to express your understanding of the links to the literature.

By enabling a clear and deeper understanding of learning and practice development, the processes of writing should enhance critical practice, which is itself a process of self-inquiry and, at times, transformative change. Our next chapter looks at these ideas more closely.

*FURTHER READING*

**Cottrell, S** (2003) *The study skills handbook*. London: Palgrave Macmillan.

A handy reference guide to thinking, learning, research, reading and writing skills for academic study.

**Watson, F, Burrows, H and Player, C** (2002) *Integrating theory and practice in social work education*. London: Jessica Kingsley.

A clear and instructive text gives practical advice on how to write better essays or assessments and give better presentations within social work, aimed at diploma level study.

# Chapter 7
## Developing critical practice

Our aim in this chapter is to focus on more critical approaches to practice rather than particular methods and techniques. Everyday social work obviously deals with risk, complexity, and contingency, and so:

- there will be range of 'solutions';

- things will change;

- outcomes cannot be predicted with utter certainty;

- certain values and assumptions may not be valid in the future;

- there will be many other perspectives on a situation.

Working with uncertainty, by allowing for contingency and checking up on how things are going, is more likely to lessen its threat and its ability to make us feel defensive. We need practices that allow us to accept and deal with ever-changing situations creatively, rather than practices that make us follow prescriptions. It is, therefore, useful to consider critical thinking for practice within its widest and most holistic sense as 'being critical' or 'taking a critical stance' and this involves a practitioner's overall approach to their work.

To do this we will explore how practitioners develop their expertise and professional judgement, but also gain the understandings and open mindset necessary to approach the uncertainty of practice in a positive way. We then look pragmatically at where criticality fits within these ways of working.

First, we can examine how practice is developed over time. Many of these ideas are based on Fook et al.'s (2000) research on the development of expertise.

# New practice

Once qualified, or indeed when taking up any new post or starting a placement, a practitioner's professional development and learning start to centre on a range of work-related aspects and knowledge.

> *The most obvious relates to a particular workplace setting or activity system and is bound up with the systems' rules, tools, norms, objectives, divisions of labour and communities of practice.*

(Knight et al., 2006, p32)

Beginning to deal with this type of 'how to' knowledge is where a practitioner's ignorance becomes obvious and can cause anxiety. It may well be the reason why many new qualified workers take a very prescriptive, rule-based approach to ensure they do not do anything wrong. In many ways such a focus on detail and correctness ensures that practitioners can be more critically aware of what they are doing than experienced workers who have established routines.

The key for workers in these situations is to attain a balance between the need for certainty and the need to be aware of other ways of doing, or thinking about, practice. Here is where critical reflection (especially involving others) can play a key role in developing confidence through the analysis of strengths-based practice, but also allow consideration of alternative options, viewpoints, etc., within a safe space, and ensure that a blinkered and uncritical rigidity does not get established.

Good critical thinking should evolve alongside a person's development within their practice. However, there is an important issue to take account of. The aim of many critical methods is to create doubt and critique of ongoing actions – we therefore cannot undertake them as a set of explicit and separate exercises because it is not possible to act confidently and thoughtfully while doubting oneself at the same time (Van Manen, 1999). We can, however, adopt critical practice more as an acceptable way of 'being' by undertaking tasks in positive and confident, but also open and flexible ways. To achieve this is it is necessary to embed criticality as an approach within professional and experienced practice itself, rather than use critical methods as remedial 'bolt-ons', which are more likely to suffer when workloads rise.

We look first at the dangers of developing in practice uncritically.

# The dangers of more experience

On a day-to-day level there are dangers associated with the development of expertise in practice. Any practice can easily fall into purely intuitive and routine methods that are followed because they are safer and less time-consuming. We develop rules of thumb and standardise our approaches to problems in order to survive our workloads. However, these habitual practices are more difficult to keep under critical control and they tend not to adapt to new circumstances easily.

In these situations uncertain problems may be 'pretended' to be certain so we can accommodate them into existing practices or our value systems, or they are simplified by ignoring certain difficult aspects. Matching similarities is easier than acknowledging dissimilarities because they confirm rather than deny our generalisations and so fit our existing knowledge. As human beings we tend to give more credence to viewpoints that are close to our own, and tend to devalue or reject information that conflicts with our beliefs. This saves time and energy and makes us feel less threatened because knowledge relies for its verification on belief, but eventually the process of evaluating our work becomes lost.

As we become less subject to dissimilarity and surprise, our experiences become non-learning situations, as we don't notice what is actually happening. So even though we have more experience in a particular environment we do not automatically acquire more valid knowledge.

In this respect, the main benefits that our post-qualifying students report when undertaking our programmes are that they:

• provide reassurance of good practices already being undertaken via discussion with others and use of the literature; but they also

• enable them to stop, think, and reassess their practice, which allows them to see where they have fallen into pure routine and adopt more appropriate methods and approaches.

Learning new knowledge, talking to others, sharing ideas, applying and connecting them to practice, and then reflecting on what happens, engages the brain in a different mode. Post-qualifying and other CPD programmes can encourage better quality approaches through their content and assessment, plus allow the opportunity and encouragement to undertake more critical work practices.

# Embedding criticality

If we look at a more positive model of expertise we can see how the holistic notion of professionally developed practice requires a critical overall disposition or stance, and also where critical thinking can be embedded as an approach to enhance existing practice.

Research adapted from Cust (1995, cited in Macaulay, 2001) shows how experienced practitioners (or 'experts' as they call them) encounter new situations.

They:

• are in control of their thinking – i.e. aware of, understand, self-direct and self-evaluate it throughout;

• have clusters of 'tacit knowledge' which form 'patterns' and represent the learning and generalising from previous experiences, from research and theory;

- recognise other meaningful patterns and principles, and irrelevant aspects, in a situation and link to these existing known patterns;

- and so gain an intuitive grasp of it;

- while assessing it in depth;

- in order to select 'schemas' (patterns or outlines formed in the mind);

- which when adapted to the problem;

- are likely to effectively represent it as well as suggesting solution procedures;

- but will periodically check to review and progress and evaluate outcomes.

Such 'experts' are seen to focus initially on the holistic assessment of a situation, rather than on explicit reasoning and analysis. In other words, they have established the necessary intuitive links to bring the different parts of a situation into a meaningful whole, to allow it to make sense for them. Each situation they face may be different but they will recognise enough of the parts to make general sense of the whole, in order to start to deal with it. Schön (1983) explained this by stating that experienced practitioners know how to define the nature of the problem or situation first – they can more easily 'name and frame' a situation.

---

ACTIVITY **7.1**

*Start to link the use of our critical resources (knowledge, critical concepts, standards, strategies, or habits of mind) to the various elements of 'expert' practice seen above.*

**COMMENT**

*It can be recognised that much of our practice and expertise, plus the thinking behind it, is of a tacit nature and will therefore be difficult to acknowledge or make explicit at times. Nevertheless, there is a need to become more aware of it (using the knowledge and concepts of critical thinking) and also to check, review and evaluate it (using the standards and strategies we have seen), by developing 'critical' habits of mind. More specific linking and embedding is explored below.*

---

## Embedding critical thinking and developing holistic critical approaches

If we now list the key expert practice areas gathered from the ideas above we can begin to see where relevant critical thinking activities can be most appropriately and positively embedded. As we can see in Table 7.1, ideas associated with professional judgement and practical reasoning are pertinent here and have been incorporated as well.

**Table 7.1** Elements and activities of critical 'expert' practice

| 'Expert' practice areas | Embedded critical thinking |
|---|---|
| 1. *Awareness, control and evaluation of thinking processes* | Thinking about thinking (meta-thinking).<br><br>Recognising and questioning arguments, etc.<br><br>Identifying and challenging own and others' assumptions. |
| 2. *Developing clusters of knowledge* | Keeping up to date; reading the literature.<br><br>Integrating values and experience.<br><br>Holding views based on valid experiential evidence but seeking and accepting relevant but alternative viewpoints and perspectives.<br><br>Generating and evaluating practice-based knowledge. |
| 3. *Assessment of situations in depth – 'naming and framing'*<br><br>*Selection and adaptation of 'schema' or framework that fits* | Gaining alternative perspective/s or reframing a situation.<br><br>Understanding when more information and input is required, knowing where and how to get it.<br><br>Lateral/creative/flexible thinking; problem forming and solving. |
| 4. *Decisions leading to action* | Decision-making and planning; use of discretion; responsibility; risk assessment.<br><br>Seeking out and taking proper account of all stakeholders' input.<br><br>Thinking through the means–end relationship as well as the implications of decisions and actions.<br><br>Predicting possible outcomes, allowing for alternatives. |
| 5. *Monitoring progress and evaluating outcomes. Adapting and changing where necessary. Ongoing learning* | Formulating clear aims/objectives at start, getting feedback and making judgements.<br><br>Using feedback and evaluation from all concerned parties, especially people who use services.<br><br>Making informal leaning more explicit.<br><br>Embedding formal learning.<br><br>Sharing and developing learning within the organisation. |

As we can see, there are many critical thinking activities that can be aligned and embedded within areas of expert practice to allow the best possible (i.e. most critical) approaches. However, it is not just about 'bolting on' a set of separate standards, strategies or methods to existing practice (although these may be important at various points). The notion of true critical practice becomes established with inherent approaches to various work practices and with holistic habits of mind – i.e. critical 'being'. For example, decisions would not just be retrospectively appraised according to a tick-box set of criteria in order to be justified; rather the process of decision-making would be undertaken with the implicit aim of identifying relevant but alternative decisions right at the start. Similarly, problem-solving would start with questioning the problem itself and gaining different viewpoints on it.

Fook et al. (2000) take this idea further. They show that practice at an expert level is not just about more knowledge and understanding from experience, but about dimensions such as creativity, artistry, openness to new ideas, and also about framing situations in complex rather than routine ways. These dimensions are associated with a process approach to practice that is committed to engaging in a particular way, rather than committed to particular or expected outcomes. A true 'expert' thus approaches any situation as a potentially unpredictable and changeable one by naturally identifying its multifaceted aspects and considering a range of options to 'name and frame' it.

The naming and framing of situations, seen earlier as the essential underlying feature of sound practical reasoning, is one major area where more critical thinking can be triggered automatically, usually by recognition of something not 'normal' – possibly an unexpected action or outcome, or an intuitive feeling of unease. This is where a critical practitioner acknowledges the difference to a usual pattern rather than ignores it, pretends it is OK, or standardises it. It is where the benefits of keeping up to date in a professional area of practice and having the necessary critical resources come to the fore. Such a practitioner will have more knowledge and awareness to recognise the incident for what it is, and more self-confidence to deal with it explicitly. The outcomes from such creative and innovative practice can result in transformative development of expertise.

This type of professional development is, therefore, not necessarily dependent on length of experience but rather on a particular disposition and mindset. Also, in this respect, we could say that such 'expertise' cannot be defined in prescriptive, narrow terms.

# Evidenced-informed practice

There is a large amount of debate concerning evidence-informed or evidence-based practice and its place within social work. It is not within the remit of this handbook to explore the arguments further and we have already looked at the critical use of formal knowledge for our purposes in a previous chapter. As students within an academic environment you will be expected to gain an understanding of the current theory, research focus and policy development within your post-qualifying specialism and discuss such issues in your assignments. As professionals we have already seen that new knowledge and ideas enhance and develop practice expertise, but your depth of involvement with different types of research material will depend on various issues, for example:

- the emphasis of your work within a medical model (which is highly evidence-based);

- the research culture of your organisation.

To sum up an overall position on this issue we could say that to apply or base practice on any type of evidence without moral or ethical sensitivity, or a wider assessment of context, individual circumstances, situational requirements, or risk assessment of possible implications would be deemed 'uncritical' practice and is unacceptable.

# Review

We do not have to pretend we are in a perfect world and always able to do the right thing. What we need to show and evidence is how we take account of the uncertainty and complexity of our role and how we try to work from a critical stance. Thinking critically must not be about feeling threatened or being made to feel inadequate. It is an holistic, open and positive way of approaching the world, and a natural one:

> *In as far as 'critical skills' go, learn to notice hunches, intuitions, gut feelings, the 'critique' is 'in there'.*

(Stokoe, 2003)

An awareness and acceptance of uncertainty in the practice of any professional is an important way to lessen stress. There are no perfect solutions out there to find, so we cannot be called on to work perfectly. If we accept the fact that the things we do or decide on are still dependent on something uncertain or on future happenings, and work in a way that takes account of that (i.e. constantly reviewing the things we deal with, decide on, or do), then this is really what 'thinking critically' is all about.

As Taylor and White (2006) show, critical practice is not about 'being certain' (the 'certain' thing is not necessarily the 'right' thing) – it is about being able to deal with uncertainty using sound, valid and accountable processes and, where appropriate, maintain a position of 'respectful uncertainty', or at least hold onto doubt for longer and seek out other possible versions.

How this stance can be used and developed within continuing learning and facilitated and enabled in others is the subject of the final chapter.

**FURTHER READING**

**Adams, R, Dominelli, L and Payne, M** (eds) (2002) *Critical practice in social work.* Basingstoke: Palgrave.

An introduction to the practicalities of social work and the principles underpinning practice, and defines critical practice in pragmatic ways for every area of social work.

**O'Sullivan, T** (2010) *Decision making in social work.* 2nd edition. London: Macmillan.

A new edition which provides a supportive framework for making social work judgements and assessments based on a structured and practical approach.

# *Chapter 8*

## Continuing learning – a critical approach

**ACHIEVING POST QUALIFYING SOCIAL WORK AWARDS**

This chapter will help you to meet the following National Occupational Standards for Social Work.
*Key role 6: Unit 21: Contribute to the promotion of best social work practice*
If you are a registered social worker, this chapter will also assist you to evidence these areas of the
Professional Capabilities Framework:
- Critical reflection and analysis
- Knowledge
- Professionalism
- Values and ethics.

We have explored where criticality fits within established ways of working to foster more critical practice. Now we can look at how it can be developed for ourselves and enabled for others within continuing learning experiences.

CPD or ongoing work-based learning can occur in many different ways (from taking part in planned, formal courses, through to informal and unplanned day-to-day encounters) and can involve our colleagues and sometimes our managers.

We will look first at maximising our own learning from all work-based learning situations; secondly at enabling criticality for other learners; and finally at social learning cultures. Some of these ideas have been drawn from, and are explored further in our book *The practice educator's handbook* (Williams and Rutter, 2010).

## Maximising ongoing learning

The type of ongoing learning required to develop skills, abilities and attributes in the workplace is multi-layered. There is no single theory of learning in the workplace and, in fact, Cheetham and Chivers (2001) point out the dangers of placing too much reliance on a single approach and argue for seeking to provide exposure to as wide a variety of learning mechanisms as possible. They encourage practitioners to view all experiences as potential learning experiences. In particular, they advocate a mindset of continuing learning from the outset in practice and collaboration with others in learning.

In this respect, practitioners who already have the skills, abilities and attributes of self-directed learners should be able to make the most of the learning potential found within work situations. Those who are lucky enough to work in a positive learning culture that encourages sharing of knowledge, plus feedback and evaluation of services, should be able to truly maximise this potential for themselves and others.

The skills of self-directed (also referred to as autonomous or independent) learning allow practitioners to:

- take the initiative in diagnosing their learning needs;

- create their own learning objectives;

- identify, locate and evaluate the resources needed;

- choose and implement appropriate learning strategies;

- evaluate learning outcomes.

These are useful skills, but, as with any process, a more holistic and critical stance can foster a deeper and more meaningful engagement. For example, here it could encourage a practitioner to actively seek and reflect on more critical feedback from service users or colleagues and gain another perspective.

Also, recognising the need to make the most of informal as well as more formal learning to develop practice becomes a critical habit of mind. Informal learning covers events like observation, feedback, dialogue and co-working, and usually results in new knowing or understanding that is either tacit or regarded as part of a person's general capability, rather than as something 'learnt'. However, it is a key area for professional development. For example, Becher (1999) reports that professionals learn six times as much through non-formal as through formal means.

To make any learning more explicit and meaningful requires a commitment to recording it, reflecting on it, actively using the ideas, etc., in practice and evaluating the outcomes. We can particularly see how our critical reflection model (see Chapter 5) could help to lift subconscious or informal learning to a more conscious and formalised level, using the critically analytical (how? and why?) and evaluative (how well?) stages. Only such conscious learning and development becomes educative in a true sense (i.e. deep, meaningful and owned), and thus able to impact on the development of professional judgement and expertise, and in turn to enhance service quality.

# Enabling others

Professional development is obviously a complex form of growth that is more than the sum of its individual parts and is never complete. A key point is that, as professionals, we will not automatically continue to learn and develop simply because we have gained more experience, or have reflected on it. As mentioned above, increasing experience may have a detrimental effect on learning as the associated increase in confidence can at times lead us into uncritical routine, where we make assumptions and fail to notice the small but possibly crucial differences between one situation and another.

Therefore, the support and facilitation of professional development and the need for social workers to play an effective role in developing other social workers (e.g. as practice educators or mentors for NQSW) becomes an important issue and is highlighted by both the Social Work Reform Board (SWRB, 2010) and Munro Review (Munro, 2011). As enablers of others in the workplace, you will need to focus on more than just 'teaching' specific practice skills and enable all levels of learners to develop not just competence but also the enhanced capability required for critical practice. This type of enablement means working in partnership with individuals and explicitly encouraging them to take responsibility for their practice (Taylor and White, 2006; Williams and Rutter, 2010). This is so much more than showing or telling someone what to do, providing answers or offering solutions (which creates dependency). It is about enabling individuals to find answers themselves. This should create flexibility and responsiveness. It is about encouraging, facilitating and supporting learners to critically explore their own practice, gain confidence in their judgement and expertise, and understand how to develop it further.

---

*ACTIVITY* **8.1**

*List some methods which you, as a qualified practitioner, might use to adopt such a critical questioning stance in order to take account of an individual learner's approach and attitude to their practice, and encourage them to take responsibility for developing that practice.*

*What differences would there be in your approach and methods between working with a qualifying student and an experienced member of staff?*

**COMMENT**

*Questions and/or learning activities should encourage and support people to think through and develop their own ideas, plus identify and explore the significance of issues and/or experiences. The idea is to get them practising working things out for themselves. Understanding what the best methods will be to achieve this can only come from getting to know them first and then working to their strengths in partnership with them. An experienced practitioner's knowledge could provide useful starting points or illustrations, and the approach taken could be as peers working together to resolve certain issues.*

---

## Appropriate methods

Open dialogue is a key element in such facilitation, and discussion can happen in many work-based scenarios, e.g. supervision, mentoring, workshops. Remember, there are no 'right' questions to ask learners because there are no clear-cut answers – 'certain' reasons and justifications are not always appropriate when talking about professional knowledge. In fact, as with any conversational situation, it is also about listening correctly (i.e. actively, without interruption or judgement) and about reflecting back what you think you've heard for clarification. McGill and Beatty (1995) recommend the use of questions that are open (e.g. how…why?), affective (e.g. how are you feeling?) and probing/checking (e.g. when…? where…? in what way…?).

Critical questioning (Brookfield, 1987) takes the dialogue process one step further in drawing out not only assumptions and underlying thoughts but also personal givens and accepted public truths. We are all imprisoned in our *own histories and constrained by the inevitable narrow paradigms of thought and action we inhabit* (Brookfield, 1987, p91). Questioning someone to elicit self-scrutiny of such issues must obviously not become, or be seen as behaviour that insults, threatens or attacks their self-esteem. It is not what you do, but how the learner perceives that action which will lead to their response. If the learner perceives questioning as threatening in any way (whether you think it is or not), he or she may retreat or attack, and the learning experience will become a very negative situation.

Critical questioning therefore involves very skilful framing of insightful and empathetic questions to encourage analysis and challenge thinking. This is a skill that may need training and subsequent refinement for qualified practitioners enabling others, but many skills may be transferred from the type of work undertaken already with service users. Brookfield (1987, pp93–4) suggests the following general guidelines:

- Be specific – relate questions to particular events, situations, people and actions.

- Work from the particular to the general – exploring a general theme within the context of a specific event helps people feel they are in familiar territory.

- Be conversational – informal, non-threatening tones help people feel comfortable.

We would add another suggestion – be emotionally intelligent, i.e. aware of the effect your questioning is having and watch for any negative signs, e.g. non-response, a defensive position being argued too aggressively, brooding resignation.

## Enabling critical refection and practice

Facilitating the critical reflection of others is obviously a difficult balance between providing a safe but appropriately challenging learning situation. As the aim of critical reflection is to create at least some doubt and critique of ongoing actions, the whole process can be extremely anxiety-provoking, especially if a learner is unsure and lacks confidence in the first place. There is another issue to consider as well which relates to criticality. Although many competency-type skills may be easily reflected on and self-appraised, a person's disposition at work and the approaches they take to work situations will be so closely tied in with their personality and previous history that for many a truly honest examination is very difficult to achieve. The requirement for critically and honestly appraising one's own assumptions, deliberations, decisions or actions requires a particular humility alongside a confident allowance of uncertainty. Obviously this is a very complex notion, especially in the early stages of a career when workers are setting out to prove themselves. The need for such honesty and humility especially holds true for the qualified practitioner if they are truly working in a partnership of trust with a learner, i.e. they have to model this behaviour in order to be credible.

If you have successfully enabled someone to critically reflect, then ensuring there are effective learning outputs from the process is the next step. Help them to scaffold and integrate the knowledge and understanding that results from critical reflection and place it into a work-based context for future use, i.e. covering knowledge, skills and values (knowing, acting and being) for practice itself. This could involve further questioning or designed learning activities, such as use of other critical incidents, imagined scenarios or role-play.

---

ACTIVITY *8.2*

*It can be rather oppressive to insist on learners following specific and prescriptive instructions to 'make' them reflect.*

*Research various models of facilitating reflection and note their common aspects. Develop your own model incorporating the features you think are most important. How can you encourage a learner to develop their own model which is specific to their needs?*

COMMENT

*A model should ensure safety as well as challenge for a learner and allow the process to be strengths-based. Most models will aim towards a form of critical analysis which can generate new understanding for future practice, i.e. something meaningful. Understanding and using their particular learning style/s and preferences should help learners create something suited to their particular approaches and ways of working.*

---

To take a wider view on enabling the critical practice of others, we can return to Taylor and White's (2006) idea that critical practice is about being able to deal with uncertainty using sound, valid and accountable processes and, where appropriate, maintaining a position of 'respectful uncertainty'. Gray and Gibbons (2007, p235) advocate that good prudent judgement is an individual virtue that must be cultivated beyond the use of structured, linear decision-making frameworks which tend to develop *the false assumption that the procedures or codes or framework will resolve the ethical problem when, clearly, there are no answers, only choices, and often the right choices make waves.*

Here, a qualified practitioner can help any learner to at least hold onto doubt for longer and seek out other possible versions as suggested. However, being adaptable enough to 'act' in a flexible manner in a wide range of circumstances is a difficult call and there may be many other methods which help foster a more open approach. What may be needed is the opportunity (with appropriate space and freedom, i.e. no risk) to explore alternative approaches and choices wherever possible. This may help reinforce understanding that there is usually more than one possible interpretation or approach to a complex situation, and that there is often no 'right answer' or 'right way' to do something in professional practice.

Enabling others to practise more critically and reflectively exposes us all to different ways of representing what we do. So the best type of work-based learning can help all participants to see their processes of reasoning and judgement more realistically and to become more reflexive, analytic and systematic in their sense-making activities (Taylor and White, 2006, p950). In other words, we may all learn from this involvement in learning; as the relative importance of learning from experience becomes greater the more expert we become. Perhaps this is a way to build true communities of practice and cultures of learning which reject the separation of training and learning from practice (Lave and Wenger, 1991) and enable the organisation to learn as well. We will briefly look at this as our next area of focus.

# Social learning cultures

There is a growing recognition of the central importance of organisations having a culture that supports continuous learning and enables the conversion of individual learning to organisational change.

We have already mentioned that the system we work in, and the people we work with, can affect our opportunities and ability to learn. Here we can look at social and environmental factors for learning effectively. Knight et al., (2006) advocate spaces for the creation of shared meaning, e.g. for collegiality and participation; and for processes such as reflection to capture, codify but also share implicit knowledge. The authors describe professional development as the development of capabilities that actually occur as a consequence of situated social practices and the work-based learning environment.

The idea of ongoing and more critical learning therefore needs to be an embedded part of being a professional social worker (as it should with any profession) and this means employers playing their full role in developing appropriate cultures and opportunities for it. Nixon and Murr (2006, p802) take the social/group learning issue further into an analysis of the role of the organisation and show that the organisational context is itself critical to the development of practice learning. They highlight how informal learning is tied up with communities of practice that can supply the social learning opportunities, and argue that practice learning makes a contribution to the quality of professional practice and the organisation's services too. Learning, therefore, does not just remain with the individual; it needs to be appropriately led and transferred in order to create the changes necessary in the organisation for improved performance.

The Social Work Reform Board's (SWRB, 2010) fostering of a culture of learning throughout a career in social work raises expectations of an entitlement to on-going learning and development. The new *Employers' Standard* reflects this entitlement for social workers to be supported in undertaking CPD through providing resources, time and access to learning and research, together with appropriate supervision. This will need to be supported by fostering a culture which values learning and development across the organisation.

Although, like previous initiatives, this will not be enough in itself to bring about a wide-scale development of learning organisations, it could help support the development of appropriate 'micro' learning cultures, in which all staff recognise and value the role that they have to play in leading and supporting individual and organisational learning.

This is obviously a huge area for debate and may be an issue you want to discuss or explore further within your programme and/or workplace.

QUESTIONS

*How can you deal with a negative work-place learning culture?*

*Which areas of professionalism are likely to suffer?*

*List any ideas that may enable you to informally lead more collaborative learning in your workplace.*

Practical ideas for developing a learning culture include:

- learning sets, e.g. for post-qualifying study;
- mentoring /coaching/induction schemes;
- engaging with projects, action research;
- staff development to encourage reflective as well as managerial supervision.

# Review

We have tried within this chapter to develop an understanding of how critical practice and the notion of capability can be developed for ourselves and enabled for others within continuing learning experiences. As work-based learners we all need directed but risk-free opportunities to critically analyse and evaluate our practice, and explore alternative approaches wherever possible, in order to deal effectively with the continuing complexity of practice.

FURTHER READING

**Beverley, A and Worsley, A** (2007) *Learning and teaching in social work practice.* London: Palgrave Macmillan.

A very readable guide to learning and teaching in social work, covering the necessary learning theory as well as the key aspects of the learning partnership.

**Gould, N and Baldwin, M** (eds) (2004) *Social work, critical reflection and the learning organisation.* Aldershot: Ashgate.

An interesting book that explores the importance of critical reflection in social work and the links between critical reflection and the creation of learning organisations.

**Williams, S, and Rutter, L** (2010) *The practice educator's handbook.* Exeter: Learning Matters.

This book aims to help practitioners develop their own, and other's, critical practice in line with the Practice Educator Standards.

# Conclusion

As we have seen, our original set of intellectual resources for critical thinking can be applied to all areas of qualifying, post-qualifying and CPD learning and be aligned with activities such as professional judgement, using knowledge in practice, critical reflection, writing and enabling self and others to develop critical practice. It comes down to three basic abilities: questioning, analysing and evaluating, which dovetail into the various methods associated with professional practice development and learning.

Critical reflection can enable the identification, exploration and understanding of practice activities, e.g. practical reasoning, decision-making, managing risk, exercising power and responsibility, using discretion, integrating values. Reflective learning will enable these activities to develop with new knowledge and new experiences. Writing critically allows an appropriate academic structuring and evidencing of this reflection for formal learning, and enables a more thorough critical analysis and evaluation of the knowledge and learning taking place.

This whole process can also constructively move our practice forward to incorporate any necessary change and development. In this way, new knowledge and understanding are developed further for ourselves, for others and for the profession itself as we begin to develop, articulate and evaluate our expertise. More holistically it develops a way of being as a professional practitioner.

We may not have a lot of time for critical thinking, reflection or writing, and, as abilities or qualities they are processes that need experience and practice in order to be undertaken effectively. PQ and other CPD learning provides the opportunities for the experience and practice, and can also give you the credit for doing it. The other good news is that you can develop your abilities by understanding the various elements involved, and by having some methods to follow, adapt and make your own. In this respect we hope this handbook has given you a better understanding, as well as some useful ideas, to work with.

Finally, good judgement, reflecting and writing skills help you to deliver good social work, as you become more able to develop and articulate the resources and services for your service users, and be accountable for them. We hope that throughout all your efforts in developing 'critical thinking' your service users will benefit.

# *Appendix*
## Harvard referencing

The following brief guidance is based on the system that Bournemouth University uses and our experience. Please refer to your own institution's regulations.

Bournemouth University, like many universities, uses the Harvard referencing system as advised in the following British Standards:

> BS 5605:1990. Recommendations for citing and referencing published material. 2nd ed. BSI. (Dorset House Library – 028.7 BRI)

> BS 1629:1989. Recommendations for references to published materials. BSI. (Dorset and Bournemouth House Libraries – 028.7 BRI)

References are cited in two different places. Firstly at the point at which a source is referred to in the text of the work; secondly in a list at the end of the work – the reference list. The following examples are all fictional and any resemblance to existing works is purely coincidental.

## Citing in the text

The Harvard system is also called the author/date method because sources are referred to in the text by giving the author's surname and the year of publication. For citations referring to particular parts of the document, the page numbers should be given after the year.

### *Examples*
(a)   Smith (2005) showed us the importance of referencing in academic work...

(b)   The five particular ways in which referencing affects academic work have been clearly explored by Smith (2005, pp24–5)...

(c)   Referencing is very important in academic work (Smith, 2005) ...

*Tip*: Many people find it difficult to remember where the brackets go. A simple tip is to think; does the author's name form part of the text? In our first two examples, the name Smith forms part of the sentence, so it is not put in the brackets (only the date). In the third example, the name Smith does not form part of the sentence, thus the author's name goes in the brackets with the date (Smith, 2005).

*Problem – no author?*

- The author (i.e. the originator) may be the organisation shown most prominently in the source as responsible for the content in its published form, so this should be given.

- For certain kinds of work, e.g. dictionaries or encyclopaedias, or if an item is the co-operative work of many individuals, none of whom have a dominant role, e.g. videos or films, the title may be used instead of an originator or author.

- For completely anonymous works, use 'Anon' instead of a name.

*Problem* – no date?

- If an exact year or date is not known, an approximate date preceded by 'ca.' may be given in square brackets , e.g. [ca.1750].

- If you can't make an approximate date then you state 'no date' in square brackets, i.e. [no date].

# Reference list

At the end of the work the references are listed in alphabetical order of originators' surnames.

*NB*: A bibliography is a list of all works that have influenced the writer of the text, not just the ones directly referred to. You will usually be asked for a reference list rather than a bibliography.

*Problem* – the same author is being listed more than once

- If you have cited more than one item by a specific author they should be listed chronologically (earliest first), and by letter (2001a, 2001b) if the author has published more than one work in a specific year.

The elements of a reference need to be in a specific order. Here are just a few examples.

## Books

> Author/originator (surname and then initials)
> Year of publication
> *Title*
> Edition (if not the first)
> Place of publication:
> Publisher.
> e.g.   Smith, B., 2005. *How to reference*. London: Bloggs Publishing.

*Problem* – the book chapter has a different author

- You make the chapter author the main originator and give the title of the chapter and its pages as well, as follows:

    Jones, J.R., 2005. Citation and plagiarism. In: B. Smith (ed.) *How to reference*. London: Bloggs Publishing, pp502–10.

*Problem* – the person you are referencing is being quoted in another work:

- In the text you must cite both authors as follows:

A study by Harris and Keeble (1996, cited in Smith 2005, p24) showed that...

but only list the work you have used, i.e. Smith, in the reference list at the end of your work.

## Journals

Author/originator (surname and then initials),
Year of publication
Title of article
*Title of journal*
Volume number and (part number)
Page numbers of contribution.

e.g.   Smith, B., 2004. The referencing nightmare. *Journal of Referencing and Citation*, 9 (1), 28–41.

## Websites

Author/originator (surname and then initials)
Year
*Title* [online]
Place of publication: Publisher (if ascertainable)
Available from: URL [accessed date].

e.g.   Smith Referencing Company., ca. 2003. *Referencing guidelines* [online]. London: Smith Referencing Co. Available from: http://www.smithreferencing.co.uk [Accessed 23 Oct 2004].

# References

**Adams, R, Dominelli, L and Payne, M** (eds) (2002) *Critical practice in social work.* Basingstoke: Palgrave.

**Alter, C and Egan, M** (1997) Logic modeling: A tool for teaching critical thinking in social work practice. *Journal of Social Work Education,* 33 (1), 85–103.

**Argyris, C and Schön, D** (1974) *Theory In practice: Increasing professional effectiveness.* San Francisco: Jossey Bass.

**Bailin, S, Case, R, Coombs, JR and Daniels, LB** (1999) Conceptualizing crtical thinking. *Journal of Curriculum Studies,* 31, 285–302.

**Barnett, R** (1997) *Higher education: A critical business.* Buckingham: Society for Research in Higher Education and Open University Press.

**Baxter Magolda, M** (1992) *Knowing and reasoning in college.* San Franciso: Jossey Bass.

**Becher, Y** (1999) *Professional practices: Commitment and capability in a changing environment.* New Brunswick, NJ: Transaction.

**Beckett, D and Hager, P** (2000) Making judgements as the basis for workplace learning: Towards an epistemiology of practice. *International Journal of Lifelong Education,* 19 (4), 300–11.

**Bloom, BS jr** (1956) *Taxonomy of educational objectives: Handbook 1. The cognitive domain.* New York: McKay.

**Boud, D, Keogh, R and Walker, D** (1985) *Reflection: Turning experience into learning.* London: Kogan Page.

**Bowlby, J** (1951) *Maternal care and mental health.* Report to the World Health Organisation. New York: Shocken Books.

**Bowlby, J** (1969) *Attachment and loss: Attachment.* New York: Basic Books.

**Brockbank, A, and McGill, I** (1998) *Facilitating reflective learning in higher education.* Buckingham: Society for Research into Higher Education and Open University Press.

**Brookfield, S** (1987) *Developing critical thinkers.* Milton Keynes: Open University Press.

**Brown, RB and McCartney, S** (2002) Multiple mirrors: Reflecting on reflections. In: R Adams, L Dominelli, and M Payne (eds) *Critical practice in social work.* London: Palgrave. pp16–31.

**Burgess, RC** (1999) Reflective practice: action learning sets for managers in social work. *Social Work Education,* 18 (3), 257–70.

**Cameron, S** (2009) *Final report from the PBPL funded project – critical engagement in the MBA.* Milton Keynes: The Open University.

**Cheetham, G, and Chivers, G** (2001) How professionals learn in practice: An investigation of informal learning amongst people working in professions. *Journal of European Industrial Training,* 25 (5), 248–92.

**Coleman, H, Rogers, G and King, J** (2002) Using portfolios to stimulate critical thinking in social work education. *Social Work Education*, 21 (5), 583–95.

**Cottrell, S** (2003) *The study skills handbook.* London: Palgrave Macmillan.

**Curry, L and Wengin, JF** (1993) *Educating the professional.* San Francisco: Jossey-Bass.

**Eraut, M** (1994) *Developing professional knowledge and competence.* London: Routledge.

**Eraut, M** (2003) The many meanings of theory and practice. *Learning in Health and Social Care.* 2 (4), 191–201.

**Fisher, A** (2001) *Critical thinking. An introduction.* Cambridge: Cambridge University.

**Fisher, T and Somerton, J** (2000) Reflection on action: The process of helping social workers to develop their use of theory in practice. *Social Work Education*, 19 (4), 387–401.

**Fook, J, Ryan, M and Hawkins, L** (2000) *Professional expertise: Practice, theory and education for working in uncertainty.* London: Whiting and Birch.

**Ford, P, Johnston, B, Mitchell, R and Myles, F** (2004) Social work education and criticality: some thoughts from research. *Social Work Education*, 23 (2), 185–98.

**Ford, P, Johnston, B, Mitchell, R and Myles, F** (2005) Practice learning and the development of students as critical practitioners: Some findings from research. *Social Work Education*, 24 (4), 391–407.

**Ghaye, A and Ghaye, K** (1998) *Teaching and learning through critical reflective practice.* London: David Fulton.

**Gibbs, L and Gambrill, E** (1999) *Critical thinking for social workers: Exercises for the helping profession.* London: Sage.

**Gibbs, L and Gambrill, E** (2002) *Evidence-based practice: Counter arguments to objections. Research on Social Work Practice,* 12 (3), 452–76.

**Gould, N and Taylor, I** (eds) (1996) *Reflective learning for social work.* London: Arena.

**Gray, M and Gibbons, J** (2007) There are no answers, only choices: Teaching ethical decision making in social work. *Australian Social Work,* (60) 2, 222–38.

**GSCC** (2005) *Post-qualifying framework for social work education and training.* London: GSCC.

**Halonen, JS** (1985) Demistifying critical thinking. *Teaching Psychology,* 22 (1), 75–81.

**Hamill, C** (1999) Academic essay writing in the first person: A guide for undergraduates. *Nursing Standard,* 13 (44), 38–40.

**Ixer, G** (1999) There's no such thing as reflection. *British Journal of Social Work,* 29, 513–27.

**Ixer, G** (2010) There's no such thing as reflection: Ten years on. *The Journal of Practice Teaching in Health and Social Work,* 10 (1), 75–93.

**Johns, C** (2000) *Becoming a reflective practitioner.* Oxford: Blackwell.

**Kandlbinder, P** (2007) Writing about practice for future learning. In Boud, D. and Falchikov, N. (eds) *Rethinking assessment in higher education: Learning for the longer term.* New York: Routledge, 159–66.

**Knight, P, Tait, J and Yorke, M** (2006) The professional learning of teachers in higher education. *Studies in Higher Education*, 31 (3), 319–39.

**Kolb, DA** (1984) *Experiential learning. Experience as the source of learning and development.* New Jersey: Prentice Hall.

**Kondrat, M** (1992) Reclaiming the practical: Formal and substantive rationality in social work practice. *Social Service Review*, 66 (2), 237–55.

**Lave, J and Wenger, E** (1991) *Situated learning: Legitimate peripheral participation.* Cambridge: Cambridge University Press.

**Macaulay, C** (2000) Transfer of learning In: VE Cree and C Macaulay (eds) *Transfer of learning in professional and vocational learning.* London: Routledge, pp1–26.

**Maslin-Prothero, S** (ed) (2001) *Bailliere's study skills for nurses.* London: Bailliere Tindall and RCN.

**Mathews, I and Crawford, K** (2011) *Evidence-based practice in social work.* Exeter: Learning Matters.

**McGill, I and Beatty, L** (1995) Continuing professional development. In I McGill and L Beatty (eds) *Action learning.* 2nd edition. London: Kogan Page, 198–208.

**Mezirow, J** (1981) A critical theory of adult learning and education. *Adult Education*, 32 (1), 3–24.

**Moon, J** (1999a) *Learning journals: A handbook for academics, students and professional development.* London: Kogan Page.

**Moon, J** (1999b) *Reflection in learning and professional development: Theory and practice.* London: Kogan Page.

**Mumm, AM** (1997) Teaching critical thinking in social work practice courses. *Journal of Social Work Education*, 33 (1), 75–85.

**Munro, E** (2011) *The Munro Review of Child Protection: Final report. A child-centred system.* Department for Education. Cm 8062. Norwich: The Stationery Office.

**Newman, T** (2000) *Developing evidence based practice in social care: Locating, appraising and using research findings on effectiveness. Guidelines for practitioners.* Exeter: CEBSS.

**Nixon, S and Murr, A** (2006) Practice learning and the development of professional practice. *Social Work Education*, 25 (8), 798–811.

**O'Reilly, D, Cunningham, L and Lester, S** (eds) (1999) *Developing the capable practitioner.* London: Kogan Page.

**O'Sullivan, T** (1999) *Decision making in social work.* London: Macmillan.

**O'Sullivan, T** (2010) *Decision making in social work.* 2nd edition. London: Macmillan.

**Parsloe, P** (ed) (2010) *Risk assessment in social care and social work.* London: Jessica Kingsley.

**Philips, V and Bond, C** (2004) Undergraduates' experiences of critical thinking. *Higher Education Research and Development.* 23 (3), 276–94

**Plath, D, English, B, Connors, L and Beveridge, A** (1999) Evaluating the outcomes of intensive critical thinking instruction for social work students. *Social Work Education*, 18 (2), 207–17.

**QAAHE** (2008) *The framework for higher education qualifications in England, Wales and Northern Ireland.* London: Quality Assurance Agency for Higher Education.

**Race, P** (2001) *The lecturer's toolkit* (2nd edn) London: Kogan Page.

**Reid, WA** (1979) Practical reasoning and curriculum theory: In search of a new paradigm. *Curriculum Inquiry,* 9 (3), 187–207.

**Rolfe, G, Freshwater, D and Jasper, M** (2001) *Critical reflection for nursing and the helping professions. A user's guide.* London: Palgrave.

**Saltiel, D** (2003) Teaching reflective research and practice on a Post Qualifying Child Care programme. *Social Work Education,* 22 (1), 105–11.

**Schön, D** (1983) *The reflective practitioner: How professionals think in action.* London: Temple Smith.

**Schön, D** (1987) *Educating the reflective practitioner.* London: Temple Smith.

**Secker, J** (1993) *From theory to practice in social work. The development of social work students' practice.* Aldershot: Avebury.

**Sheldon, B and Chilvers, R** (2000) *Evidence-based social care. A study of prospects and problems.* Lyme Regis: Russell House.

**Smith, F** (1992) *To think; In language, learning and education.* London: Routledge.

**Social Work Reform Board** (SWRB) (2010) *Building a safe and confident future: One year on.* London: Social Work Reform Board.

**Social Work Reform Board** (SWRB) (2011) *Proposals for implementing a coherent and effective national framework for the continuing professional development of social workers.* London: Social Work Reform Board.

**Sotto, E** (1994) *When teaching becomes learning: A theory and practice of teaching.* London: Continuum.

**Stokoe, L** (2003) *Critical analysis skills.* Worcester: University College Worcester. www.worc.ac.uk/departs/psycho/Teaching/Critical.html. (Accessed 7 Jan 2004.)

**Streumer, B** (2009) Practical reasoning. In O'Connor, T and Sandis, C (eds) *The Blackwell companion to the philosophy of action.* Oxford: Blackwell.

**Taylor, B** (2010) *Professional decision making in social work practice.* Exeter: Learning Matters.

**Taylor, CP and White, S** (2001) Knowledge, truth and reflexivity: The problem of judgement in social work. *Journal of Social Work,* 1 (37), 37–59.

**Thompson, S and Thompson, N** (2008) *The critically reflective practitioner.* London: Palgrave Macmillan.

**Van Manen, M** (1995) On the epistemology of reflective practice. *Teachers and Teaching; Theory and Practice.* 1 (1), 33–50.

**Watson, F, Burrows, H and Player, C** (2002) *Integrating theory and practice in social work education.* London: Jessica Kingsley.

**Weick, A, Rapp, C, Sullivan, WP and Kristhardt, W** (1989) A strengths perspective for social work practice. *Social Work,* 34, 350–4.

**Williams, S and Rutter, L** (2007) *Enabling and assessing work-based learning for social work. Supporting the development of professional practice.* Birmingham: Learn to Care.

**Williams, S and Rutter, L** (2010) *The practice educator's handbook.* Exeter: Learning Matters.

**Yelloly, M and Henkel, M** (eds) (1995) *Learning and teaching in social work: Towards reflective practice.* London: Jessica Kingsley.

# Index